D0445223

ECONOMIC GANGSTERS

ECONOMIC GANGSTERS

Corruption, Violence, and
the Poverty of Nations

Raymond Fisman and Edward Miguel

PRINCETON UNIVERSITY PRESS

PRINCETON AND OXFORD

Published by Princeton University Press,
41 William Street, Princeton, New Jersey 08540
In the United Kingdom: Princeton University Press,
6 Oxford Street, Woodstock, Oxfordshire OX20 1TW

Library of Congress Cataloging-in-Publication Data

Fisman, Raymond.
Economic gangsters : corruption, violence, and the poverty of nations /
Raymond Fisman and Edward Miguel.
p. cm.
Includes index.
ISBN 978-0-691-13454-3 (hardcover : alk. paper) 1. Corruption—Economic
aspects. 2. Political corruption—Economic aspects. 3. Smuggling. I. Miguel,
Edward. II. Title.
HV6768.F57 2008
364.1'323—dc22
2008025208

British Library Cataloging-in-Publication Data is available
This book has been composed in Goudy
Printed on acid-free paper. ∞
press.princeton.edu
Printed in the United States of America
1 3 5 7 9 10 8 6 4 2

For Ellie
For Ali

Contents

ECONOMIC GANGSTERS

Chapter One

Fighting for Economic Development

In the summer of 2004, world-renowned Kenyan novelist Ngugi Wa Thiong'o returned to his homeland after twenty-two years in exile. He flew to Nairobi to launch his new novel, *Wizard of the Crow*, his first in over a decade. Ngugi's earlier works—a dozen or so novels and collections of stories, which he began publishing just after Kenyan independence in 1963—had been wildly successful, not only in Kenya but throughout the world. Through his carefully wrought characters and achingly familiar plots of loss and suffering, Ngugi captured the bewildering contradictions left behind in the wake of European colonialism.

Ngugi had lived those contradictions and drew inspiration from his experiences, which were shared by so many of his fellow Kenyans. Ngugi had grown up during the 1950s, when Kenya had been rocked by the Mau Mau rebellion against its British colonizers. He had witnessed the murder of his brother, who had died along with thousands of other Kenyans in opposing the British. And he had celebrated with his countrymen as they watched the British imperial machinery retreat in 1963 at the birth of the Kenyan nation. He had also suffered at the hands of the second free Kenyan government—for despite the country's turn to self-rule and hopes for a bright future, Ngugi had been forced to flee Kenya in the 1980s following years of persecution and imprisonment for his sharp criticism of the post-independence regime.

Novels like *A Grain of Wheat*, published in 1967, just four years after Jomo Kenyatta became independent Kenya's first president, provided a window into the hopes and frustrations that came with the dismantling of the Western empires—dreams of economic prosperity measured against tales of corruption seeded throughout the new government. *A Grain of Wheat* is a fable about the early, tumultuous years of a free Kenya, and captures the unwavering hope for a bright future coupled with the fear of what the British legacy of corruption and violence might bring. "Would independence bring the land into African hands? And would that make a difference to the small man in the village?" asks Ngugi through the novel's main character, Gikonyo.[1]

In the 1950s and 1960s, that same question echoed in the minds of the citizens of newly independent countries from Kenya and Sierra Leone to Indonesia and Pakistan. What would the future hold? Would freedom bring jobs, peace, and wealth? The sentiment that drove these concerns would help make Ngugi's novels international sensations; they've been translated into more than thirty languages and are considered classics of African literature. For Ngugi himself, the post-independence years spent in exile had brought professional acclaim and prosperity. He had taught at New York University as the Erich Maria Remarque Professor of Languages and is now a professor at the University of California at Irvine, where he directs the Center for Writing and Translation. And he returned to Kenya in 2004 not with bitterness about the past but with optimism for the future. "I come back with an open mind, an open heart and open arms. I have come to touch base. I have come to learn," he told the crowds of well-wishers upon landing in Nairobi.[2]

But even in the face of the enthusiasm, hope, and joy that greeted his return—a visit that came not long after Kenya's longtime dictator Daniel arap Moi, his longtime persecutor, had stepped down to make way for a democratically elected government—Ngugi was brutally assaulted in his rented Nairobi apartment, beaten, his face burned with cigarettes; his wife, Njeeri, was raped. Many interpreted the attack as payback from the earlier regime for Ngugi's outspoken criticism of Kenyan politicians and politics, and served as yet another reminder of the despair and unfulfilled aspirations of Kenya's people. The parallels were made even more poignant by the widespread political violence in Kenya in early 2008.[3]

This isn't the way it was supposed to be.

Over the past four decades, we've witnessed some of the greatest economic miracles in human history. In 1963, an average person in South Korea or Kenya earned only a few hundred dollars a year. Most eked out a living as peasant farmers. Back then, it wasn't so clear where you'd lay your bets if you had to guess which country would be rich at the end of the millennium. Both countries were recovering from the devastating armed conflicts that had accompanied decolonization. South Korea had already boosted its literacy rates by the early 1960s, but Kenya had much greater natural resource wealth to exploit, including some of the world's richest soil for growing coffee, cotton, and tea.

After decades of first manufacturing textiles, then refining steel, and finally producing high-end consumer goods and advanced electronics, South Korea pulled off an economic leapfrog that today puts it among the world's wealthy nations. South Korean citizens now enjoy a standard of living rivaling the Japanese, their former colonizers, and that of many European nations. But the average Kenyan is no better off today than he was in 1963.

What went wrong? In looking back over four decades of history, what can we learn of why South Korea—and Malaysia and Thailand and now China—began to close the income gap with Europe and North America, while Bangladesh, Pakistan, Central America, and most of sub-Saharan Africa remain mired in extreme poverty?

This is the puzzle that gets the two of us out of bed and into the office each morning, and solving it is the ultimate purpose of the research that we'll share with you. This book isn't about finding *the* singular explanation for why poor countries are poor. You should probably be suspicious of anyone selling you a grand unified theory of poverty (or anything else). Human societies are far too complicated for that.

But neither do we subscribe to the view that no one can make progress on such a vexing problem. Many hard lessons have been learned since 1963. The experiences of newly independent Kenyans—the fruits of their hard labor lost to corruption or destroyed by violence—foreshadow the twin evils of corruption and violence that have been so central to Kenya's modern economic experience as to be inseparable from it. As we'll see, Kenya's story is far from unique: from the post-colonial plundering in Indonesia to the bloody civil wars of Central America and Africa, the destructive power of corruption and violence is clear for all to see.

The Lives and Times of Economic Gangsters

Al Capone is remembered as a gangster and a brutal, cold-blooded killer. It is perhaps less widely known that Capone was also an accountant for a Baltimore construction firm before joining and eventually leading Chicago's North Side Gang.[4] We don't normally associate the relatively humble and perhaps humdrum vocation of bookkeeping with mob icons like Capone. There are no scenes of Al Pacino struggling to balance the books or poring over financial statements in the films *Scarface* or *The Godfather*. But Capone's training as an accountant was instrumental in helping him organize a vast criminal business empire. The emphasis was on *business*—it's just that Capone's business happened to be in prostitution, gambling, racketeering, and selling booze during Prohibition, illicit trades where disputes were settled with machine guns rather than lawyers.

According to biographer Robert Schoenberg, Capone was "a businessman of crime [with] lucid, rational, and discoverable reasons for his actions."[5] He is the quintessential economic gangster: a violent and lawless criminal who wrought havoc on 1920s Chicago, but did so in a rational, calculating way.[6] A cold-blooded killer, yes, but violence was simply a tool Capone used to keep the money rolling in.

5

The pathological cruelty of gangsters like Capone makes them particularly repellant—they're guilty of crimes of calculation, never passion—but also the source of endless fascination. Yet their narrow self-interest, driven by money and power, makes them more understandable to economists, not less. It's not that we economists do not realize how important emotions can be in governing behavior (we are in fact people too). But the side to human behavior that economists choose to study is embodied in the species *Homo economicus*, or Economic man—a rational, self-serving being whose actions and choices are based on logical decisions, not rash impulses. If the criminal mind, like Capone's, really is very close to the self-serving ideal in our models, then economic analysis can be a useful tool in figuring out how to combat corruption and other forms of lawbreaking.

There's good reason to believe that the characters that populate this book—from the despotic warlords of sub-Saharan Africa to the smugglers of the South China Sea—do indeed obey the logical laws of economics. To understand why, it's useful to think about what keeps you from cheating a little on your taxes, or slipping out of a restaurant without paying the bill. It's in part a fear of the legal consequences if you get caught. But the punishment of tax cheats is rare and usually light, and you could stiff a waiter his tip without risking any legal penalties (although you may not be welcome back at that particular restaurant). Yet most people still do the right thing most of the time. Probably more than fines or jail time, what constrains us from breaking the law is the fact that it just isn't right. We're constrained by conscience.

But antisocial personalities like Capone were blessed with relatively few such encumbrances. So if anyone is going to behave in their narrowest self-interest—by cheating on taxes or restaurant bills, or even killing off business rivals to earn a few dollars more—we would expect it to be a criminal character unconstrained by scruples, what we call the "economic gangster." And as we'll see, there's a bit of economic gangster in each of us. When placed in desperate circumstances all people are reduced to the rational calculus of survival, with conscience a forgone luxury.

The goal of this book, and the research it's based on, is to understand the havoc wrought by the corruption and violence of the world's economic gangsters, and to place their impacts on economic development in sharper relief. (To appreciate the problem, imagine what life would be like under Mayor Capone of Chicago or even President Capone. Unfortunately, many people in the developing world don't need to use their imaginations to grasp what it means to be ruled by thuggish bandits.)

While we certainly don't have all the answers, in our research odyssey to make sense of corruption and violence over the past decade, we have uncovered some amazing facts—and surprising solutions.

We are researchers and professors in development economics at U.S. academic institutions (Ray at the Columbia Business School and Ted at the University of California, Berkeley). But our research forces us out of the ivory tower to get a closer look at the real world. Our economic detective work has taken us from remote Kenyan villages to the floor of the Indonesian stock exchange for new angles on the sources of global poverty. Unexpected answers about corruption and violence are found in the most unlikely of places: in tales of smuggled Chinese chickens, diplomatic parking tickets in Manhattan, and even Tanzanian witch-hunts.

This book brings together the lessons we've learned by

marrying economic analysis with the insights gained in our expeditions through the rural back roads and glittery new skyscrapers of the developing world. We hope these lessons can, in some small way, help Kenyans and the rest of the developing world finally realize the economic aspirations they hold for themselves and their children.

It's not an overstatement to say that the question that we confront—how best to fight global poverty—is of epochal importance. The well-being of most human beings is at stake. Recent World Bank calculations estimate that a billion people live on less than one dollar a day, while half the world's population—about three billion—gets by on a daily income of less than two dollars.[7]

How do people survive on so little? The answer is brutally simple: not well. Hunger plagues daily life for hundreds of millions, and health care is scarce or nonexistent. In war-torn Chad, Niger, and Sierra Leone, adult literacy rates still hover under 30 percent, and children have a better chance of dying before age one than they have of graduating from high school.

Global poverty matters a lot even to those Americans (and other privileged citizens of the Western world) who generally have little regard for what goes on beyond their own borders—even if they aren't conscious of it. As we'll see repeatedly throughout this book, we're all stuck with one another on this planet. Poverty breeds desperation and discontent: we wake up daily to headlines of terrorist threats, environmental degradation, and other global ills that find their origins in Middle Eastern slums and the rainforest clear-cuts scarring the Congo River basin. Tackling the problem of global poverty is an imperative for the entire world, both rich and poor.

Hope For a New Generation?

International economic development returns to the public eye in the United States every few years. Lately, renewed interest in Africa's plight in particular has been fueled by the star power of Angelina Jolie and U2's Bono, combined with devastating images of the HIV/AIDS epidemic and genocide in Darfur, Sudan. We hear pleas for debt relief and more generous international aid from America and Europe. Entrepreneurs like Bill Gates and Warren Buffett are spending tens of billions of their own dollars to fight malaria, treat AIDS, and educate Africans, to ultimately "make poverty history."[8]

But we've been here before. Our generation had its LiveAid concerts and "We Are the World" albums following the horrific 1984 famine during the Ethiopian civil war—star power (there's Bono again) mixed with the iconic image of a starving child left to die on the dusty earth. Private charities and countries' foreign aid agencies have spent billions annually for decades now hoping to wipe out poverty. We've seen round after round of debt relief since the 1970s. But despite all this the average Kenyan is still no richer today than in 1963. Will things really be any different this time around?

Well-informed people hold widely divergent and passionate views on this fundamental question. You might think economists mainly spend their time engaged in emotionally inert conversations on the niceties of monetary policy or crunching numbers on next month's inflation (and this does describe what many economists do). Yet these otherwise mild-mannered, monotone academics have almost come to blows over the question of why foreign aid to developing countries seems to have failed so spectacularly.

9

Fundamentally, it boils down to whether rich countries have already provided too much money to help Kenya and others out of poverty—or not nearly enough. Leading academic researchers have lined up on both sides. The answer turns out to hinge critically on one's views of the role that corruption and violence play in the impoverishment of nations. Maybe corruption and violence are mainly just the symptoms of poverty. If this is the case, once rich-country donors finally send enough money to Kenya to jump-start economic growth, its citizens will no longer have to fight one another to survive. On the other hand, if most foreign aid is lost to the grabbing hands of corrupt officials or destroyed in civil strife, then how could aid dollars ever lift countries like Kenya out of poverty? More aid would just enrich an already corrupt elite, and could even make the twin problems of corruption and violence worse by giving people even more money to fight over.

These questions are central to understanding the current foreign aid debate and the inflamed passions of development economists (including ourselves), and are an underlying motivation behind everything else that follows in this book. Before we dive into our own new findings, though, we'll introduce you to the broader debate that lurks in the background. Hundreds of scholars are engaged in the full-time study of global economic development, but many fit into two main camps whose views are captured by two leading development thinkers.

Jeffrey Sachs, director of Columbia University's Earth Institute, is a tireless public campaigner for more international development assistance. Sachs was a professor at Harvard when we were getting our economics PhDs there, and we were both fortunate to experience his academic brilliance and rhetorical talents firsthand. He is that rare thinker whose observations can leave you feeling like you understand the world a little better after every conversation. And in the world of socially awkward professors that we inhabit, Sachs's charisma is legendary. Ted was actually inspired to do development work in Africa during graduate school, in part, by one of Sachs's mesmerizing speeches on the moral dimensions of fighting global poverty.

Sachs is the leading proponent of the "poverty trap" view of economic growth. The idea behind a poverty trap is simple. A poor Kenyan farmer cannot easily rise out of poverty on his own. He can't afford to buy adequate food to nourish his family or to send his children to proper schools, and any savings he may salt away from a good year will quickly be wiped out by a bad harvest or disease the next. The farmer's destitution almost guarantees that he and his children will remain destitute. And so on, over the years.

In Sachs's view, foreign aid is the sudden jolt that can lift a farmer—or village or entire economy—out of this cycle of poverty-induced poverty. There's a catch: building health clinics, improving schools, and adding infrastructure like roads and power generators for a whole country or continent is expensive, and by Sachs's reckoning, the foreign aid budget of the United States would need to increase at least five-fold to pull the developing world out of its poverty trap.

As laid out in Sachs's recent best-selling book *The End of Poverty*, Kenya is poor because we in the rich world aren't spending nearly enough to help them out, but if these resources were available poverty could be eliminated from our planet in short order. Sachs argues that "the wealth of the rich world . . . make[s] the end of poverty a realistic probability by the year 2025."[9]

Sachs's ideas for ending poverty make sense in theory. But many other economists hold the opposite view, that we're spending *too much* on foreign aid already—or at least spending it in all the wrong ways and places. Bill Easterly is the public face for these arguments. Since being forced out of the World Bank for publicly slamming its foreign aid policies, Easterly, now a professor at New York University, has become the primary spokesperson for the view that aid has done very little good overall for the world's poor. He claims that *trillions* of U.S. dollars have already been wasted by the World Bank and other donors, and that Sachs's plan of expanding aid five-fold would likely fritter away trillions more. Easterly argues that these enormous sums of aid money have often been spent on grandiose, centrally planned projects—hydroelectric dams, four-lane highways, desalination plants—in countries ill-prepared to oversee their construction, operation, and upkeep.

Easterly compares the approach of most foreign aid donors to that taken in the 1950s by Soviet economic planners, who dreamed of a new economic order where wise Moscow bureaucrats would perfectly anticipate and meet the needs of all workers and peasants. But, he asks, how can foreign aid central planners, parachuted in from Washington D.C., really know how to make distant economies develop? How did they know that Kenyans needed hydroelectric dams rather than new universities? Why more highways than irrigation ditches (or vice versa)? And even for programs that were designed to build desperately needed schools or health clinics, how could the donors be sure that Kenya's leaders actually used the money as intended—and didn't steal it or spend it on something else entirely?

What we do know today is that much of the developing

world doesn't have a lot to show for these past foreign aid efforts, barely anything beyond a collection of rusting monuments to good intentions. Trillions of dollars were wasted on roads to nowhere or power plants that never lit up a single home. Billions more were stolen. To add insult to injury, the world's greatest economic miracles have occurred in countries—including both China and India, both of which had African-level poverty as recently as the 1980s—that largely spurned the advances of the big foreign aid institutions. If these two economies have managed to expand at record speed for decades without meaningful foreign aid, why is a big push from foreign aid really the right remedy for Kenya, say? Why not follow in China and India's footsteps instead?

Easterly and his fellow "institutionalists" contend that before we multiply our foreign aid budgets five-fold, we need to make sure the recipient countries can really use these extra dollars. Countries receiving aid money need to be well-governed and someone needs to keep watch to make sure the money is spent to serve the interests of the "common man" rather than The Man in the president's mansion. Aid recipients should have well-functioning government institutions and civil society organizations, like media and community associations, that will hold the government accountable, and prevent economic gangsters from coming to power.

Many developing countries are far from this ideal. Until they fix up these so-called institutions, Easterly argues, the best we can do is fund small-scale social entrepreneurs—what Easterly calls "Searchers" in his recent book, The White Man's Burden—who find innovative solutions to local development problems.[10] Such small-scale interventions can be monitored and held accountable by donors and the community even in the midst of generalized central government corruption. If successful they could be scaled up to benefit even more people. As societies find ways to deal with corruption and disorder, people in poor communities will feel more comfortable investing in their own futures, and economic development should follow. But until then, we shouldn't throw good money after bad.

Everyone likes a good fight (especially Sachs's and Easterly's book publisher). But these two points of view are not completely at odds. Sachs and Easterly are two very smart people. Sachs isn't advocating that donors direct-deposit billions of dollars into the Swiss bank accounts of corrupt dictators, or bring them briefcases full of unmarked hundred dollar bills and hope for the best. And Easterly isn't suggesting that we in the rich world completely abandon poor countries to their collective fate, waiting stubbornly for them to get their houses in perfect order before writing any checks at all.

Yet critical distinctions separate them. Sachs's poverty trap view holds that we need to pull people out of poverty first and then pretty much everything else—good government, an active media, and community participation in politics—will follow. But the first step is making sure the poor no longer have to worry about where their next meal is coming from.

Easterly's opposing perspective counters that this would be putting the cart before the horse. We've tried the economic "big push" before to the tune of trillions of dollars over decades, and Africa is just as poor as it was in the 1960s. An even bigger push by foreign aid planners could simply result in even more money lost to misuse and abuse (and greater disillusionment among potential future donors).

Both prescriptions for how best to help poor countries are plausible. But to evaluate their respective merits, we need to better understand corruption, violence, and the motivations of the economic gangsters who are responsible for so many past development failures.

A Walk on the Dark Side of Economic Development

Neither of us started our careers as economists with the intention of spending our lives researching human depravity. In the beginning, we only wanted to better understand why poor countries were so poor and what could be done about it. Yet the concurrence of violence, corruption, and persistent poverty is so pervasive that it is almost impossible to separate the study of poverty from these other social ills. So we've each spent over a decade now thinking and writing—and sometimes even dreaming—about corruption, violence, and poverty, and we've made it our life's work to understand exactly how they're related.

Because all three often appear hand in hand, figuring out where we should focus our efforts is a classic chicken-and-egg problem, and one that is intimately connected to the Sachs-Easterly debate. If countries first deal with corruption, will economic growth follow? Or should donors pull countries out of poverty first before they can ever hope to deal with violence and corruption? Both views are reasonable, but for now they're just theories. What we really need are better real-world answers.

That's where our research and this book come in. Our main objective is to understand the intricacies of the corruption–violence–poverty chicken-and-egg question using cold hard facts rather than rhetoric. The foundation of what follows is our own research from academic economics journals (sometimes based on work with other coauthors whom you'll meet as well). To bring new evidence to the debate, we apply the tools and insights of economic analysis to data that we've carefully collected over years working in Asia and Africa. We believe that the developing world's best hope is to base policy decisions on rational analysis rather than ideology.

In the chapters that follow, we'll tell six stories—three on corruption, three on violence—that have started to breach the barriers to understanding violence and corruption in the developing world. These stories take us on journeys to the hidden and often chaotic worlds of economic gangsters. From massacres in Vietnam to the container ports of Hong Kong, in remote African villages to the streets of midtown Manhattan, the answers come in far-flung and rather unusual places, and also in unexpected ways.

For better or worse, we humans seem to have an innate interest in corruption, violence, and other mortal sins. The questions we're asking, and the back doors we discover in our search for answers, hold a fascination in and of themselves, and we'll show you the latest tools and tricks of the economics trade along the way. Beyond our Mafia tales and war stories, you'll see that the brand of economic sleuthing we use is closer to Sherlock Holmes than C-SPAN.

As we'll see, the answer to the chicken-and-egg problem of poverty and violence can, quite literally, fall from the sky in the form of rain. To measure the value of political ties, we use a massive betting pool where investors wager billions on the value of connections. Is corruption a matter of conscience, culture, or fear of punishment? Answers can be found in the expired parking meters around New York City's United Nations Plaza.

Throughout the book we take our research lessons and draw out their practical implications for foreign aid and other debates on how best to fight global poverty. In the process, and particularly in our concluding chapter, we'll introduce some new ideas for helping the world's poorest citizens achieve their economic aspirations. By the end of the book, we hope you'll see the potential that economic research has in helping to really make poverty history.

Counting Invisible Chickens and Eggs

If so many people care so much about global poverty, and violence and corruption are important pieces to solving the puzzle, you might wonder why we don't already have all the answers. Why haven't we already resolved whether corrupt governments and violence undermine economic growth, or if poverty creates the conditions for civil conflicts and thieving bureaucrats?

The problem is that chicken-and-egg problems are hard to resolve—that's why we have the phrase "chicken or egg," so we can wave our hands at a problem and move on. But we can't just wave our hands at global poverty. Later in the book we'll describe the tragic history of Chad, one of Africa's poorest countries. Recent decades have seen a near-continuous sequence of political upheaval, violent civil wars, government theft, and economic decline. But which came first, the wars or the economic collapse? They're both happening at the same time so it's hard to know for sure. Or perhaps the fighting is caused by something else entirely, like political rivalry between Christian and Muslim Chadians. In that case, the root cause we need to address is ethnic conflict. But so much is happening at once—political battles, rising ethnic tensions, environmental degradation, diversion of the country's oil wealth, worsening poverty—that we start to feel like a dog chasing his tail in trying to figure out what's really going on.

Besides, this is all assuming we have enough information to argue ourselves in circles to begin with. Before trying to understand whether violence and corruption cause poverty or vice versa, we first need to know how much violence and corruption is actually out there. Corruption—Transparency International defines it as "the illegal use of public office for private gain"—is something which by its very definition takes place out of sight.[11] If bribe givers and takers are doing a halfway decent job of it, there's no obvious paper trail of what took place. Bribes don't appear in companies' tax returns, nor are they reported to shareholders in annual reports or cash-flow statements.[12] So we're now trying to solve a chicken-and-egg problem where we can't even see the chickens (or the eggs).

But if we can't see bribe payments taking place, we could try asking people about them directly. We could talk to company officials about their back-alley deals, or ask the bribe-takers in government about how much they are bringing in on the side. Yet given the legal consequences, there are good reasons to believe that responses to the question, "How much did you pay last year in bribes?," are of questionable accuracy.

In general, we economists are skeptical of what people *say* on any topic. We call it "cheap talk," since words don't need to be backed up by money or actions. And we're particularly suspicious of cheap talk on sensitive topics like bribe payments and embezzlement. This is obviously true for those directly involved in illegal payments—the givers and takers of bribes—but we also don't put too much stock in the opinions of the supposedly disinterested experts who might estimate the bribe payments made by others.

Suppose, for example, we're trying to figure out how much Tarique Rahman, son of the former Bangladeshi prime minister, collected in bribes from foreign companies in 2005 (we'll take up the closely related question of what it's worth to be the president of Indonesia's son in more detail in chapter 2). If you survey informed Bangladeshis on this matter, you'll end up with a number that could be much higher or much lower than the actual amount the First Son pocketed, depending on whom you ask. It's obvious, really. People's stated opinions reflect their unstated agendas and biases. When asked, supporters of the former Bangladeshi government will naturally downplay the extent of corruption in the First Family, while opponents might inflate the scope of the problem. Similarly, the main objective of business owners in answering a corruption survey is to stay out of prison, and hence they are likely to underreport their own bribe payments.

And that's the heart of the problem: we humans often say what we *wish* was true rather than describing things as they actually are. Let's take a little test: What kind of coffee do you like? As noted by author Malcolm Gladwell, the odds are that right now you're thinking you love a dark, hearty roast.[13] Yet when most people put in their morning order at Starbucks, they choose a thin, milky cappuccino. Somehow the dark roast fits with the self-image many of us have as robust, adventurous drinkers (and people). The problem is, hearty roasts just don't taste very good. So we may claim our

19

preferences are one thing but reveal very different preferences when called to action.

Finally, opinions disproportionately reflect people's own personal experiences. During visits to the allegedly corrupt country of Bangladesh, Ray never observed policemen shaking down passersby for cash. At worst, he witnessed them milling about looking bored and smoking cigarettes when they probably should have been out directing traffic. Similarly, there were no overtures by airport customs officials to have their palms greased in exchange for allowing Ray to leave the country. So if you ask Ray—or other similarly privileged foreign visitors—Bangladesh doesn't seem corrupt at all. If we extrapolated from Ray's own positive personal experiences, the whole corruption problem would seem totally overblown.

Rather than only listening to what people *say*, we need to see what they *do*. If Nescafé wants to know how you really like your coffee, they're much better off running blind taste-tests than asking you to fill out a form. And if we want to know how much people are taking in bribes in Bangladesh, we have to find a way to overcome the cheap talk problem and follow the money.

Say "Cheese"

One way of getting a "real" measure of corruption is to arm yourself with a hidden camera, pose as a shady arms dealer, and see if you can catch politicians red-handed on tape. The FBI actually did this in the late 1970s, creating a phony company called Abdul Enterprises to solicit favors—including assistance in laundering money—for a fictitious wealthy Middle Eastern oil sheik. Undercover FBI agents offered cash to senators, congressmen, and other U.S. politicians, all with the tape recorder running. This so-called "Abscam Operation" resulted in convictions of five congressmen, a senator, and numerous local officials, and caused a public uproar over apparently rampant corruption in the U.S. government.

The media can substitute for the FBI in countries where governments are less inclined towards self-examination. The Indian magazine *Tehelka* pulled off an Abscam-like exposé in 2001. In an elaborately staged deception, a pair of journalists posed as representatives for a nonexistent London-based company, West End, hoping to sell night-vision cameras to the Indian Army. The journalists caught senior government officials and army officers on tape taking bribes or discussing the mechanics of making bribe payments. These revelations, broadcast to the world via the Web, rocked India for weeks. In the wake of the scandal, and perhaps in part as retribution, *Tehelka*'s offices were raided on multiple occasions and several of its journalists wound up in prison.

As tempting as it might be, in this book we leave these sensationalist methods—and the opportunity to get an insider's perspective on Indian prisons—to others, and instead employ the tools of the economics research trade to uncover corruption. A challenge, to be sure, but as we'll see starting in chapter 2, some briefcases of cash leave footprints we can follow.

Chapter Two

Suharto, Inc.

What's it worth to be the president's son? Ask the average Indonesian and he'll tell you it's worth a lot—a whole lot. Based on what he saw under former President Suharto, it was enough for Suharto's son, Mandala Putra Suharto, to pay for multimillion dollar vacation homes scattered about the globe, a fleet of fancy cars, and other playboy indulgences. The exploits of Tommy, as he's known, were standard fare in local tabloids and provided everyday Indonesians with a window into the privileged lives of their First Family. Tommy driving around Jakarta in his Rolls Royce; Tommy attending a celebrity-studded black tie dinner; Tommy with his latest supermodel girlfriend—so *that's* what being the president's son is worth!

Where did Tommy get the cash to pay for his fancy cars? Like the other Suharto children, Tommy was a businessman, and his corporate empire touched every facet of the Indonesian economy, including companies that rolled cigarettes, broadcast television, manufactured automobiles, and pretty much everything in between. Tommy's seeming Midas touch meant that his companies generated big profits, and he wasn't shy about taking his share. His personal net worth was estimated at $800 million by the mid-1990s.[1] Though perhaps less conspicuous in their spending, his brother Bambang and sister Tutut amassed similar fortunes.

Did Tommy and the other First Children owe their business successes and wealth to their connections to the country's president, who also happened to be their father? The man on the street would certainly say so. Suharto family members had a reputation for demanding a cut of any company wanting to do business with the government. That's how the kids got their fingers in so many pies. From electric power projects to roads to timber, someone in the president's family saw a piece of the action. The Suharto family firms also did remarkably well in securing government contracts: Tommy was handpicked to spearhead government-subsidized efforts to develop a "made-in-Indonesia" national car, and one of Tutut's companies won the bid to build toll roads through the capital, Jakarta.

Their father, not surprisingly, held a very different view of his kids' success. While Tommy and his siblings may have gotten a little paternal guidance to get started, he thought their accomplishments were the result of business savvy, hard work, and disciplined management. After all, Indonesia's economy grew at an astonishing 6 percent per year over the three decades of Suharto's rule. Surely this wouldn't have been possible under a corrupt system that valued connections over competence?

Who should we believe? How many of Tommy's millions came from his skills as an investor and manager and how much from an indulgent father's handouts? What's it *really* worth to be the president's son? In the absence of hard evidence, we're left with two opposing opinions. And as we've already learned in chapter 1, cheap talk often differs from underlying realities. In figuring out the answer to this riddle, we'll try to cut through all the cheap talk and let cold hard cash do the talking.

Before we go hunting around for solutions to the problem of corruption, it's worth thinking about whether there's a problem to begin with.

How much corruption is there, really? The answer surely depends on both time and place (America today versus America one hundred years ago; Sweden versus Indonesia). What we find will matter in deciding how much effort to devote to dealing with corruption instead of other social problems, and also whether or not to keep sending foreign aid dollars that might end up lining the pockets of crooked politicians.

Real Measures of Corruption—Letting the Markets Speak

If talk is cheap, especially when it comes to corruption, we need some other mechanism for revealing what people really know. Ideally, we could ask everyone to bet some of their own money on whether a particular company was making back-alley deals with politicians to get lucrative government contracts. Those with the inside track on the relationships the company had cultivated with politicians would bet a lot; those without privileged information would choose to bet less, or not at all, since, in effect, they'd just be guessing. In this political betting pool, raw financial self-interest drives bettors to reveal their true beliefs about corruption. But clearly this isn't a bet offered by Vegas bookmakers or others. As it turns out, though, this betting pool is strikingly similar to the stock market, where investors essentially gamble on whether they think corporate profits will be high or low.

A stock, or "share," represents very literally the ownership of a tiny piece of a company. For example, Amazon has around 414 million shares outstanding, so owning one share means you control 1/414,000,000th of Amazon, the main benefit of which is your claim to 1/414,000,000th of Amazon's profits. Suppose that Amazon's stock price was a dollar, and that you expected the company to make profits of $414 million dollars, or one dollar per share, every year for at least the next decade as internet sales replace corner bookstores. Then, for a mere dollar, you can buy the right to annual profits of a dollar for at least ten years—a pretty good deal.

If this is really what you believe, then you and everyone else with the same views on Amazon's future profits should be on the phone to your brokers buying more Amazon stock from other stockholders with less optimistic views of Amazon's future. On the other hand, the internet revolution notwithstanding, Amazon sometimes makes pretty close to zero profits because of the very high cost of distributing books, and this may not change anytime soon. If this is what you think, your dollar's worth of ownership doesn't get you much at all, so if there's a sucker out there who will buy your share of Amazon for a dollar, you (and everyone else who thinks like you do) should be selling whatever Amazon shares you currently own. If most investors think that the value of future profits will be high relative to the share's purchase price, we'd see lots of buyers and few sellers at the going price, which pushes the stock price up; if most investors think profits will be low, their selling drives prices down.

In reality, there's a constant flow of information on Amazon's business situation that forces investors to rethink whether they should be buying or selling the stock, and investors react accordingly. For example, if UPS announces that it's raising the cost of book delivery, which eats into Amazon's profits, then selling by investors will drive Amazon's stock price down. Because of this daily deluge of updates and the differences of opinion among investors in how to interpret the news—How much of the UPS price hike will Amazon be able to pass on to its customers? How much of what we read in the morning paper is rumor versus reality?—prices bounce around a lot. A share price reflects investors' consensus view of future profits—the invisible hand of the market at work—and this collective wisdom of thousands of well-informed buyers and sellers is captured by the daily ups and downs of stock prices.

How does this fit into our corruption discussion? Recall the West End Corporation (WEC) discussed in chapter 1 that was set up by journalists to sting politicians and military brass by trying to bribe its way into selling night-vision cameras to the Indian army. Suppose that WEC's value without the camera contract is one dollar per share but that the extra sales from night-vision cameras would double WEC's profits. That means that the value of the company's share will double to two dollars if and when they get the contract.

Now think of the briefcase of cash passed to an influential politician as an "investment" that WEC makes today to lock in the night-vision camera contract. If no one is aware of this investment, then WEC's share price remains at a dollar until the contract is announced, at which point a buying frenzy will push the price up to two dollars to reflect the expected profit increase.

But if we wind back the clock a little to the briefcase handoff, while most of the world thinks WEC shares are worth one dollar, company insiders already know that the company will be worth two dollars in the very near future. Those insiders—WEC's CEO, for example, or a good friend who was tipped off, or the friend's friend who also got news of the deal, or the politician (and *his* friends) who took the cash and is poised to choose WEC for the contract—can trade a dollar for a share that will soon be worth two dollars, so why not buy now and make a profit? In fact, why not keep buying and buying until the price hits two dollars per share? As a result, in-the-know investors push the price of WEC shares up toward two dollars even before the announcement. Insiders reveal their knowledge of the company's value through their purchases of WEC shares, and this gets revealed to the rest of the market through the doubling stock price.

If you suspected something was amiss and asked the CEO's buddy (or the buddy's buddy) why he was buying up WEC shares at $1.50 apiece when it would seem they're objectively worth only one dollar, odds are he won't tell you about the briefcase of unmarked bills. He may mumble something about his confidence in WEC's senior management and superior product line to create value and higher future profits—he'd treat you to a dose of cheap talk because the truth is completely illegal.

It's Not What You Know . . .

So the market tries to put a value on everything that might affect companies' profits, including things like bribes and political ties. When there's big money on the line, investors think hard about whether to buy or sell.

How can we use this insight to figure out how much corruption there is in Indonesia or anywhere else? There are plenty of companies in Indonesia with high share prices. Is this because they've invested in political ties that lock in lucrative government contracts—or because they have really smart executives and high-quality products? Or maybe it's a little of both: executives that are skilled in cultivating political ties may also be good at making and marketing merchandise.

What we'd like to do is observe which companies delivered briefcases of cash to parliament and measure the return on their investment, which would tell us how much extra profit firms generate for each dollar spent on political favors. Most of us will never observe the inherently unobservable under-the-table payment and be able to calculate the corporate profits that are generated as a result. But thinking about business-political connections so narrowly, and solely in terms of cash payments, fails to do justice to the ingenuity of modern finance and the broad range of tools to which builders of political bridges may avail themselves.

So instead of giving Tommy Suharto or one of his siblings bundles of unmarked bills, you can just give him a million dollars' worth of shares in your company. In exchange, Tommy could help ensure that you win valuable logging concessions, obtain tax holidays from the revenue authority, and otherwise make sure you get at least a million dollars' worth of corporate value out of his government connections. Through family ties, campaign finance, and personal friendships, companies around the world are able to purchase government connections that we *can* observe. So while we can't *directly* answer the question, "How much do firms pay in bribes?," as we'll see, we can do a pretty good job with a very similar question: "What is the value of companies' political connections?"

We in the United States have a number of homegrown examples of companies that would appear to be suspiciously intertwined with government officials. Most prominently, Dick Cheney left his job as CEO of the energy services giant Halliburton to join George W. Bush's presidential ticket in 2000. During the election campaign, concerns of corporate favoritism emerged, concerns that only intensified with the lucrative no-bid contracts awarded to Halliburton during the Iraq War.

It's worth noting, however, that rebuilding the oil infrastructure of a war-torn nation actually *is* rocket science, so to speak: it takes more than a set of power tools and a copy of *Oil Drilling for Dummies* to compete with Halliburton. So it may be that Halliburton was the most deserving recipient of contracts awarded by a government scrambling to deploy resources in Iraq, and Cheney's Halliburton ties are merely a coincidence.

We'll return to the Cheney example later to see if Halliburton's profits really were tethered to Cheney's political fortunes, or if it was actually a case of guilt by association. But our Dick Cheney and Tommy Suharto examples should give you an idea of where to look in our hunt for politically connected firms: tycoons-turned-politicians, as in Cheney's case; former politicians and government officials who have taken up lucrative corporate jobs; and in the case of Tommy and the other Suharto kids, politicians' friends, relatives, and colleagues. But finding politically connected companies is just the start. Here comes the hard part: figuring out what these connections are worth.

All the President's Children: Born Smart or Lucky?

In his book, *In Praise of Nepotism*, Adam Bellow (son of Nobel literature laureate Saul Bellow) argues that the business and political legacies of the world are usually justified on meritocratic grounds. The rich deserve to pass on their positions of influence to their kids because, the Bellow fils argues, these captains of industry and government provide both the "nature" and "nurture" to shape their progeny into similarly capable leaders (just as great writers will surely produce articulate sons and daughters).[2] If great leaders beget great leaders, then we shouldn't be surprised to find that the companies of presidential offspring are very profitable.

But what if our statistical analysis shows us that well-connected companies aren't that profitable after all? Should we conclude that bankrolling a presidential campaign buys you nothing more than a night in the White House's Lincoln Bedroom? That's also not so clear: presidential favors might not come cheap. Imagine that you'd like to get into the oil drilling business. There are two types of investments you can make. You can buy cutting-edge technology and hire an army of MIT engineering grads to ensure you're the most efficient driller in the industry. Or you can spend lavishly, courting politicians and hiring an army of Washington lobbyists to be sure you'll be at the head of the queue for any new drilling concessions.

These two strategies might produce similar profits but they generate value in totally different ways, and they also differ in their vulnerability to upheaval in the competitive landscape. We'll exploit these vulnerabilities—in a research sense—to measure how the market values political connections.

This is how it works. Suppose you choose the high-tech approach to building your business, while an upstart competitor works the political angle. What will happen to your respective profits if a hurricane blows through the Gulf of Mexico, destroying both your rigs and those of your connected competitor? Your profits will plummet: your fancy and expensive gadgetry now sits at the bottom of the ocean. By contrast, your competitor's business, built on cheap rigs but costly political connections, will be much less affected. His sunken rigs weren't that valuable to begin with and he'll probably work his political ties to get a government bailout through disaster relief funds. Your stock price will plunge while your competitor's remains more or less unchanged.

Now suppose the political equivalent of a hurricane tears through Washington D.C. The president, undone by scandal, suddenly leaves office, severing your competitor's carefully cultivated connections. With his political investments rendered valueless, future prospects look dim and the decline in expected profits will lead to a similar drop in his share price triggered by an investor sell-off.

Both of these hurricane scenarios share one crucial element—*surprise*. Markets are generally unmoved by happenings that are old news or events that unfold slowly. The effects have already been incorporated into prices by the trading of forward-looking and knowledgeable investors, as in the case of the WEC shares that were bid up even in advance of the government contract being signed.[3]

Our search for a market value of connections will essentially be a search for political hurricanes. We'll hunt around for episodes of *unexpected* political upheaval and measure how the values of politically well-connected companies are affected by these shifts. Those price differences will show us what connections are worth. Although political turnover is common enough, some kinds of political change will work better for our purposes than others. In the 1972 U.S. election, for example, political pundits had Richard Nixon as the heavy favorite over George McGovern from beginning to end. So when financial markets opened on November 8, the day after Nixon's landslide win, investors didn't blink. Even before the results were announced, everyone had been doing their buying and selling with the expectation Nixon would stay in the White House. Our recent 2000 presidential election, by contrast, was a nail-biting, up-to-the-last-minute affair where investors were awake through the night (and sometimes for weeks afterwards) wondering who would sit in the Oval Office.[4]

But we'll go beyond surprise election results to make our corruption analysis work. It will be most useful to begin our search for the value of political connections in the countries where corruption is most prevalent. Vigorous democracy is relatively rare in such places, and close races in rigged elections rare indeed. And, in their own way, dictatorial regimes built around a single individual are sometimes even more hurricane-prone than democracies. The unexpected death, illness, or removal of a dictator abruptly cuts off the flow of favors to the politically connected. Our approach for measuring the value of political connections thus takes us on a morbid quest for unexpected changes in the health and well-being of political leaders. The sudden death of a politician potentially provides exactly the political hurricane we're after.

"Whenever Mr. Suharto catches a cold, shares in Bimantara Citra catch pneumonia"[5]

Our search for political hurricanes takes us back to Indonesia under President Suharto. His regime had its roots in a 1965 power struggle between Indonesia's military and its civilian government. When the smoke had cleared, a young and relatively unknown General Suharto emerged as the country's de facto leader. In March 1966 he made his position official, taking the title of Acting President. A year later Suharto, who like many Indonesians went by a single name, was elected president, a position he held for over thirty years.

Every aspect of political and economic life felt Suharto's influence: his government allocated subsidies and trade protections to promote strategic industries, provided low-interest loans through government-owned banks, and presided over a host of licensing restrictions that determined, among other things, who could grow oranges, roll cigarettes, cut down trees, build toll roads, and import rice. The long arm of the Suharto regime essentially dictated who would make money and how much. It was this power that, in the eyes of many Indonesians, allowed Suharto's children and others with close Suharto ties to become so fabulously wealthy.

Armed with ideas from this chapter, we now have a means to get to the root of our original question: What's it worth to be the president's son? And more generally, what was the value of having connections to the Suharto regime? Investors on the Jakarta Stock Exchange (JSX) will provide us with an answer. Many well-connected businessmen owned very large stakes in companies traded on the JSX, including Tommy Suharto's own media conglomerate, Bimantara Citra. But there were also many JSX companies that managed to do business without strong connections, including the palm oil and real estate companies of Aburizal Bakrie. While not totally lacking in connections, Mr. Bakrie was better known for his entrepreneurial acumen than his presidential politicking.

How much did it matter to Bimantara Citra to have Tommy on board? Since Tommy's value presumably comes from the link to his presidential father, any indication that Suharto might not be around much longer should hurt the company's stock price. By looking at the decline in value of well-connected companies like Bimantara Citra in response to bad news about Suharto's health, and comparing this with the decrease (or increase) in value of companies with weaker political ties, like Bakrie's firms, we can compute a market value for connections to the president.

Clearly, the biggest shock to the value of political ties, and the cleanest case for our research, would have been Suharto's sudden demise. None of his kids or cronies were seen as capable successors, so whoever else eventually took over would be unlikely (or unable) to honor all of the political connections cultivated under Suharto. No such luck (for the analysis). Suharto didn't die while in office. But he was well into his seventies by 1995, and began to experience health problems with greater frequency. Where his death had earlier been a distant hypothetical, by the 1990s his longevity became a matter of intense speculation. Articles started appearing in the financial press reporting on possible illnesses. The stories that emerged during 1996 turned out to be mere rumors, but the tremors that ran through the Indonesian business community hinted at the unease that many investors felt about the coming regime change.

On July 4, 1996, a government announcement sent the

JSX tumbling: Suharto was traveling to Germany for a health check-up. That may not sound like much, but who travels ten time zones to get his pulse taken? Investors at the stock exchange were inundated with rumors that Suharto had already suffered a stroke, or might be headed to Frankfurt for emergency heart surgery. The Jakarta Composite Index (JCI), an indicator of Indonesian stocks' overall performance, much like New York's Dow Jones Index, fell by 2.3 percent on the day of the news.

What was merely bad for Indonesian stocks turned out to be devastating for Bimantara Citra and its boss, Tommy Suharto. Just how damaging? It's clearly visible in the plot of Bimantara's stock price, which we show along with the level of the overall JCI in figure 2.1. You can see that in the weeks leading up to the July 4th announcement, both the JCI and the price of Bimantara Citra bounced around a bit, not gaining or losing very much. Then, with the market awash with rumors on July 4th and 5th, Bimantara's stock price took a nosedive: the prospect of a connectionless Bimantara had shareholders dumping their shares and running for the exits, driving its price down by more than 10 percent in just two days.

The following week, Suharto's German doctors gave him a clean bill of health. The reports of imminent bypass surgery turned out to be pure rumor-mongering, and all of Suharto's test results looked good (in fact he didn't die until the early winter of 2008, when we were putting the finishing touches on this chapter). With its connections now more secure, for the moment at least, Bimantara shares all of a sudden looked like a relative bargain. Investors went on a buying spree and Bimantara's share price jumped back up—although not quite back to its pre-checkup levels. The Germany trip had clearly reminded investors that Suharto and

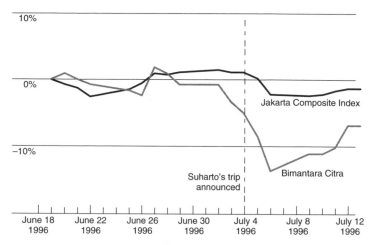

Figure 2.1: Change in the value of Jakarta shares during Suharto's
1996 trip to Germany

his regime couldn't last forever, making them that much
more cautious about the long-term prospects for Bimantara
Citra's political ties and profits.

The Collective Wisdom of Insiders

If you examine figure 2.1, you'll notice another curious pattern in Bimantara Citra's stock price. Recall that the government announced Suharto's Germany medical trip on July
4, 1996. But in the two days before the announcement, Bimantara's stock was already in a fairly steep slide, down about
5 percent from its earlier levels. The collective wisdom of
investors seems to have foreseen that Suharto would seek
German medical attention a full two days before it was announced. How could that be?

A lot of money was on the line. If you had known on July 2nd that Bimantara's price would start its free fall on July 4, you could have sold your shares for a much higher price than what you would have gotten for the same shares just two days later. Certainly Suharto's doctors knew about the upcoming trip, so you can guess they were dumping any Bimantara shares they held personally. The same could be said of those lucky investors who were friends with Suharto's medical team or inner circle. The most well-connected investors presumably got to trade early on the news about possible changes to Bimantara's political connections.

It isn't necessary that everyone knew that Suharto was headed to Germany. It's enough for the insiders to trade on their special information to get the stock price moving in the right direction. Trading on proprietary insider information by corporate executives and their friends is, of course, illegal in the United States and many other countries, including Indonesia, and is punishable by jail time. Among the many charges leveled against Jeffrey Skilling, former president and CEO of Enron, was that he sold shares in the company when he knew its stock price was dramatically inflated. By selling early, he made over $15 million on the sale of Enron shares that were nearly valueless only a few weeks later. Such is the power of inside information.

Ray experienced the power of the Jakarta whisper network firsthand while working on his doctoral thesis in December 1997. He spent months wandering from office to office amidst Jakarta's gleaming new skyscrapers, talking to the occasional investment banker or journalist willing to spend some time with a lowly graduate student. One morning, he had secured an appointment with Rick Borsuk, a reporter for the *Asian Wall Street Journal*. But the meeting didn't really go as planned—Borsuk's phone scarcely stopped ringing during the abbreviated interview. The stock market had gone absolutely berserk at the opening bell, trading on rumors that Suharto had suffered a stroke and might even be dead. The feverish speculation was apparently set off by claims that medical equipment had been surreptitiously delivered to the presidential compound overnight. Everyone had already heard this story by the opening bell. Shares in Tommy Suharto's Bimantara Citra again dropped, this time by 22 percent, while shares in his sister's company fell 17 percent. The lesson was clear: the market was keeping its finger on Suharto's pulse, so to speak, and if it ever skipped a beat prices responded sharply.

The earlier German trip on July 4th for medical tests triggered selling in many other Suharto-connected companies. On average, share prices of companies owned by the Suharto inner circle dropped by about 4.5 percent on those days. By contrast, share prices in Aburizal Bakrie's connectionless companies actually jumped up a little on the news, gaining over 1 percent, and leading to a nearly 6 percent difference between the effect of Suharto's illness on the well-connected and the unconnected. So, 6 percent of the expected profits of well-connected companies disappeared overnight, all because of a health checkup! Investors have spoken through their trading actions: even the mere endangerment of political ties moves markets (a rumor of a stroke, while serious, is very far from death).

On five other occasions between 1995 and 1997 Suharto health rumors surfaced, albeit less serious ones. In every case, the share prices of Bimantara Citra and other connected companies took a beating, while shares in the less-connected companies of Mr. Bakrie stayed flat, or eked out small gains. The market, in its rational-minded way, was telling us over and over again that political connections in Suharto's Indonesia mattered *a lot* for corporate profits.[6]

Exactly how much did these connections matter? We never experienced the event that many Indonesians were bracing themselves for: the sudden death of their oppressive dictator. But we can generate an estimate of the total value of connections based on the market's response to Suharto's various medical ups and downs, which suggests investors believed that about one quarter of the value of politically well-connected companies would be lost if Suharto's regime came to an abrupt end.[7] How big is 25 percent of company value? When Apple announced its iPhone to great fanfare in 2006, Apple shares went up by 8 percent, and when Pfizer was unexpectedly forced to withdraw Trovan in 1999, marketed as the antibiotic of the future, Pfizer shares fell by 10 percent. So, connections are worth a lot more than a blockbuster new drug or the next big technology gadget, or even both of them combined.

Corruption in Suharto's Indonesia wasn't some petty shakedown by underpaid policemen or labor inspectors trying to make ends meet. It was big business. In Indonesia, corruption started at the very top and cascaded downward. What chance of success might an anticorruption crusade have in such an environment? The market has told us that Indonesia's connected business elite were making fistfuls of cash under Suharto's system of political patronage. Those who were best positioned to change a corrupt system liked it fine just the way it was.

Given the system's benefits to Indonesia's insiders, it should come as no surprise that political and economic reform had stalled and that serious reform attempts materialized only at the end of Suharto's rule. As the Asian financial crisis erupted in late 1997 and Suharto still clung to power, the IMF tried to impose some discipline on Suharto's cronies. As a condition of the IMF relief package, state-sanctioned monopolies were supposed to be dismantled and government-owned banks were to stop funneling money into well-connected businesses. But Suharto effectively killed these attempts at reform. Nor could the Indonesian people appeal to the democratic process. While national elections were held periodically, Suharto's Golkar party never failed to reach its targeted vote share of 70 percent. Once his own election was rubber-stamped by the friendly parliament, the Indonesian constitution gave Suharto near total power.[8] Unfortunately, in the face of such a totalitarian regime, evidence from economics research on the extent of corruption won't by itself help very much in bringing about reform. We researchers can throw light on the problem, but this information must be accompanied by popular political pressure on leaders themselves.[9]

Tommy Suharto's $40 Million Pocket Money

Tommy Suharto loved cars. Especially fast cars, and Lamborghinis in particular. In fact, he loved them so much he bought the company. In 1994, Tommy bought a controlling stake in the Italian sports car manufacturer for $40 million. As the new owner, he soon took an active role in planning and operations. Perhaps not impressed by his automotive and management expertise, a number of top executives soon quit, leaving a management vacuum at the company. Nonetheless, the *Wall Street Journal* reported in 1998 that Tommy's stake in Lamborghini was sold at a significant profit, even under the distressed circumstance facing Tommy after the Asian financial crisis. So, was the Lamborghini purchase a frivolous investment financed by Daddy's money? Or a calculated purchase by a savvy investor with expertise in fast cars? Based on our findings, it appears that Indonesian investors thought much of Tommy's value came more from connections rather than business smarts.

Is All Corruption Created Equal?

The story of Suharto's rule in Indonesia also raises the uneasy question of whether outsiders should do anything about corruption at all. Despite the apparent large-scale skimming by the Suharto regime, the country managed a remarkable 6 percent rate of economic growth over the thirty-two years of Suharto's reign, making it one of the great economic success stories of modern history. (By comparison, the United States grew at a little more than 3 percent per year over the same period.) While the Suharto clan may have taken more than its fair share, poverty rates fell dramatically in the Suharto years, and public education, health, and family planning programs were also greatly expanded. Plenty was left over to trickle down to everyday Indonesians.

As we emphasized in chapter 1, corrupt countries do not grow quickly *in general*, but Suharto's Indonesia was an exception. Perhaps foreign donors like the IMF should think carefully before tinkering with an arrangement, albeit a corrupt one, that worked so effectively over a span of three decades. But how did a corrupt system grow so fast for so long?

There are a few possible explanations. Maybe companies favored by Suharto, in addition to being well connected, were also well run. Going back to our oil drilling metaphor, maybe they were run by a partnership of Washington lobbyists and MIT engineers. Or maybe Suharto made sure that stealing never got totally out of hand. Recall that we estimated that 25 percent of companies' profits came from connections, *not* 50 or 100 percent. And for better or worse, the Suharto regime had a reputation for holding up its end of bribe transactions, at least removing the uncertainty that is a natural part of most illicit dealings. In the words of one foreign executive with decades of business experience in Jakarta, "there was a price for everything and everyone knew the price and knew what he was getting for what he paid." By contrast, the same executive lamented that in today's post-Suharto Indonesia, "you see chaos instead."[10]

At the same time, Indonesia might have grown even quicker in the absence of corruption. For a hint at what might have been, take a look at South Korea, a purportedly less corrupt Asian Tiger that grew even faster than Indonesia in the decades of Suharto's reign. For all his faults, Suharto did bring draconian discipline and stability to a country that had earlier been in chaos, and it's difficult to second-guess what might have been without his leadership. In the decade since Suharto's fall from power, a vibrant democracy has emerged but it has yet to achieve the economic growth rates experienced under Suharto's corrupt dictatorship.

But this probably shouldn't change our overall stance on reducing corruption. Few highly corrupt countries have had the economic successes of Suharto's Indonesia. But it does muddy the waters a little on what we have to say about the benefits of rooting out corruption. Policymakers and foreign aid donors like to have simple prescriptions for action, but unfortunately the world is complicated and ambiguous. When does corruption still allow for economic miracles like Indonesia, and when does it bring about economic stagnation or decline, as seems to be the case in much of sub-Saharan Africa? As corruption researchers, we don't yet have ready answers. But we're starting to come up with the right kinds of questions. Does it help to have corruption organized under a strong dictator such as Suharto (see textbox)? Is corruption less damaging if bureaucrats and politicians are secure in their jobs, and hence can guarantee that "the goods" will be delivered as promised? Now that economists have begun to develop better ways of measuring corruption, we can use these tools to try to understand where corruption wreaks the greatest havoc, and ultimately also help Indonesians and others do something about it.

The Benefits of Organizing Crime

Leonardo "Narduzzo" Messina, a seventh generation mafioso from southern Sicily, was arrested by Italian authorities in April 1992. He soon began informing on his past associates, providing details on the structure of the modern Mafia. The picture that emerged was one of an increasingly centralized crime bureaucracy, with local bosses passing on profits earned through their protection rackets and narcotics sales to the big boss in the Sicilian capital of Palermo. The local dons were kept honest, so to speak, by "ambassadors" from the central office sent to ensure that tributes were paid and that the local bosses didn't tread on one anothers' turf.

This centralized organization served the Sicilian Mafia well. According to Messina's testimony, the mob was making so much money that it couldn't possibly all be laundered, so they rented an apartment in Palermo—the "House of Money"—to store big bundles of banknotes. As you can imagine, many poor shopkeepers and small businessmen resented their monthly hundred-dollar contributions to the mighty stacks of bills littering the House of Money.[11] But perhaps they should have been counting their blessings instead. Economic theory predicts that the level of extortion under a centralized and well-coordinated Mafia system should be lower than would be the case with an uncoordinated free-for-all, with local bosses simply looking out for themselves.[12] Similarly, the companies paying tributes to Suharto, Inc., were probably paying smaller bribes in total than if they'd had to pay off officials from a bunch of uncoordinated ministries (the labor ministry, environment ministry, and potentially a host of others).

To understand why a coordinated shakedown leads to lower rates of extortion, consider the situation faced by a small Sicilian shopkeeper (let's call him Signor Grasso). Under a centralized bureaucracy (an "organized crime" syndicate, if you will), Signor Grasso should receive only one monthly visit from a Mafia enforcer to collect protection money.

SUHARTO, INC.

How much should the Mafia charge Signor Grasso for the privilege of staying in business and remaining alive? A higher price brings in more revenue to the mob, but also risks driving Signor Grasso out of business—at some point, the extortion payment gets so high that the poor shopkeeper might simply shut down and find some other way to earn a living. So if the big boss in Palermo is smart, he'll pick an intermediate price for "protection" that doesn't scare off Signor Grasso or too many of Sicily's other small business owners.

Suppose that the Italian police decide to take down the big boss, and there's no longer anyone to coordinate the Mafia's racketeering operations. Now Signor Grasso may receive two visits each month from local bosses—call them Vito and Fredo—each separately demanding protection money, and each thinking they deserve the amount that Signor Grasso had been handing over to the big boss. But they have to take into account the trade-offs involved. When Don Vito stops by for his monthly payment, he thinks about the trade-off between a higher level of extortion and the loss of income if Signor Grasso goes out of business. But what he fails to consider is that if he sets his extortion rates too high, he'll also be taking away some of Don Fredo's business when he stops by later for his monthly take (and in fact by *not* raising his rates, he may think that he's just leaving money on the table for Don Fredo). Because Don Vito fails to account for the full cost of raising his extortion rates, he will set his prices "too high." The same goes for Don Fredo—he doesn't think about his effect on Don Vito in choosing his protection rates.

As a result, the Dons each set a price that is too high, and end up killing off more businesses relative to the orderly corruption of the earlier big boss era. The Mafia makes less money, and the few shopkeepers who remain open spend more on bribes than they did back in the day, when crime was truly organized.

The same lesson may hold for Indonesia: the centralized corruption of Suharto, Inc. may have resulted in lower total bribe payments for firms relative to the post-Suharto scramble for bribes by individual ministries, with each squeezing as much as possible from each company without considering the impact on other ministries' rackets. It's yet another reason that corruption under Suharto's iron hand, while not necessarily a boon for business, may not have wrought the sort of economic devastation it has elsewhere in the developing world, where power is less tightly centralized and many economic gangsters jostle for bribes.

Corruption in Indonesia, and Thailand, and Italy, and . . .

Our attempts to measure the value of political ties began in Indonesia, but doesn't end there. Suharto's government was seen as one of the most corrupt dictatorships on the planet in the late 1990s, when the events we study took place. So it's not fair to make broad, sweeping statements about high-level corruption in regimes whose bureaucracies may be corrupt on a lesser scale, or in more democratic societies. We can, however, take the same approach we've used for Indonesia to study corruption around the world.

We can't do this anywhere or anytime we like, though. All of the conditions we saw in Indonesia must be met. First, we need a country with an active stock market to observe investors' bets on the value of political ties. Few African countries have enough large companies to support well-functioning stock markets, so we can't study them using this approach (we will measure corruption in Africa using an entirely different method in chapter 4, though). And even in somewhat richer countries like Malaysia, stock markets only came of age in the 1990s. We also need a good measure of companies' political ties, so we need some way of tracking business-politics relationships. This is easy in Thailand and Italy where politicians themselves also run the country's largest corporations, but is trickier (though not impossible) in countries like the United States where there is at least a nominal separation between business and politics. Finally, we'll need unexpected events—political hurricanes—such as surprise election outcomes or a politician's sudden illness or death that alter the value of political ties.

Economics researchers, most notably, Mara Faccio, a finance professor at Vanderbilt University, have applied this method around the globe.[13] To get a comprehensive political connectedness index, she's followed the political careers of business tycoons (as well as the business careers of politicians), traced blood lines to detect family ties, and read the society columns of local newspapers to find out who dines

with whom. Her most striking observation is the preponder-
ance of close political-corporate ties in most countries. In
Russia, fully 87 percent of the Moscow Stock Exchange's
value is in companies with close Kremlin ties. Maybe this
isn't such a shock in the "Wild West" capitalism of post-Soviet
Russia. More surprisingly, nearly 40 percent of the London
Stock Exchange is politically connected. And as Professor
Faccio observes, her approach misses some political ties, so
these are underestimates.

The existence of personal connections linking business
and politics doesn't necessarily imply favor giving. Maybe
high-level politicians use the same leadership skills that
served them well in government to become successful businessmen. Or maybe successful people from many different
fields—government, business, the arts, sports—all tend to
gravitate to one other socially. So we again need to look for
ways to estimate the value of these connections. Faccio focuses on unexpected election outcomes and announcements
of political appointments, a somewhat less morbid way of
documenting political ties than our Suharto study. Rather
than contemplating Suharto's sudden death, imagine that a
democratic Indonesia unexpectedly handed the president an
electoral loss instead of his usual 70 percent vote share.

With Professor Faccio's findings in hand, we can figure
out a market-based value of political ties in a larger set of
countries. While business-politics connections are very common in the United Kingdom, Professor Faccio finds that
when these ties are unexpectedly strengthened, the stock
prices of affected companies don't budge. So, for example,
when Rolls-Royce Chairman Sir John Moore was appointed
to the House of Lords, there was no detectable effect on
Rolls-Royce's stock price. In Faccio's native Italy though,

true to the Hollywood stereotype, insider connections do matter. The Italian Senate appointment of Fiat boss Giovanni Agnelli boosted his companies' stock prices by 3.4 percent, which translates into many billions of dollars in additional value.

The British have found a way to reign in political favor giving while the Italians haven't. Perhaps the bruising British tabloid press is effective in keeping bad behavior in check; maybe it's the efficient court system; or perhaps it's individual conscience borne of a British sense of propriety. Now that economists have come up with the value of political connections worldwide, we must also try to account for these differences, a task we'll return to in chapter 4.

Business and Politics as Usual in Washington, D.C.

Beneath all the media talk about corporate interests controlling Capitol Hill, do current U.S. political leaders look more British or Italian? This is a centuries-old question. Corruption in the U.S. Congress has been the source of partisan and populist hand-wringing since it became illegal to bribe congresspeople in 1853. Before this, their conduct was regulated by an internal set of rules on decorum and debate. Voting on matters where a member of Congress had a conflict of interest was illegal. So was spitting, cursing, and any other behavior that threatened the Congress's reputation and honor. (Incidentally, no one ever got the boot for conflict of interest or bribe-taking, but one congressman was nearly expelled for violating the no-spitting rule in 1798.)[14]

To be sure, it would seem that outright cash bribes are rare these days.[15] But has this old-fashioned cash-for-favors exchange simply been replaced by a system that trades political influence for campaign financing, international "business trips" on corporate jets, and highly paid post-government employment?

At the same time, we Americans have many civil society organizations, like the Center for Responsive Politics and Judicial Watch, that report on campaign finance and related matters. We have an army of investigative journalists who report regularly on business involvement in politics. Our two-party electoral system should provide political competition and accountability. All of this keeps business-politics relations in the public eye, and hopefully keeps our politicians honest and influence peddling in check.

How much of a priority should Congress make curtailing influence-seeking by companies and lobbyists? Is it worth spending time fighting this battle at the expense of, say, expanding health care or social security reform? The answer clearly depends on how much influence is *actually* being bought and sold on Capitol Hill, not as a matter of opinion but as a matter of fact.

To get these facts, we can again see what investors think about the matter. Washington, D.C. is a veritable petri dish for economics researchers trying to evaluate political connections. The generous campaign giving and lobbying by corporate America (and wealthy individuals) is all a matter of public record, and the revolving door in and out of government generates a steady flow of businesspeople into politics and vice versa. Further, we've witnessed some very unexpected political events in recent years—the cliffhanger 2000 presidential election; Vermont Senator Jim Jeffords's surprise decision to become a Democrat in 2001; Dick Cheney's unstable heart—that give us shocks that we can use to compute the value of all manner of political connections. Finally, the New York Stock Exchange and the NASDAQ are the biggest investor casinos on the planet, with thousands of companies' stock prices to study.

The cottage industry of economists and political scientists studying political connections finds that the spotlight of media exposure has *not* been sufficient to sanitize Washington, D.C. politics. Politically connected companies in the United States often make a lot of money from their government ties, whether measured by personal connections or by political giving. For example, when Jim Jeffords crossed party lines and handed control of the Senate to the Democrats, Democratic donors benefited and Republican donors suffered.[16] And when the Supreme Court decided that George W. Bush would be elected president in 2000, companies with former Republican lawmakers as board members increased in value; those with former Democratic lawmakers on the board declined.[17]

A curious exception is the notorious case of Dick Cheney's Halliburton ties. If the vice-president were indeed as instrumental as some claim in ensuring profitable federal government contracts for Halliburton, the company's investors should have felt their own hearts skip a beat each time Cheney got his heart checked, and his heart attacks (November 2000 and March 2001) and blood clots (September 2005 and March 2007) should have made them *very* anxious. Yet each time, the Halliburton stock price barely budged in response to Cheney's personal health ups and downs, and none of the other companies with personal ties to Cheney have ever responded much to his personal fortunes.[18]

It looks like there are limits to favor giving in Washington: lower-level politicians can sometimes get away with giving favors to friends, and ex-politicians may be effective at securing political assistance for corporate clients. As vice president, though, Cheney's every decision was intensely scrutinized by numerous watchdog organizations and media outlets spanning the ideological spectrum, and their frequent warnings of potential conflicts of interest may in fact have helped to limit his favor giving, rather than reveal it. Or maybe Haliburton is so well connected it need not rely on any single politician, no matter how powerful.[19] Or maybe Dick Cheney just isn't personally corrupt after all.

The United States is not as corrupt as Indonesia, where President Suharto himself presided over an all-encompassing system of "relationship capitalism" where connections were everything (or at least 25 percent of everything). But we in the United States also seem to fall far short of countries like the United Kingdom in keeping money out of politics. So at the risk of getting distracted from other important public policy issues, it looks like we're right to keep worrying about business and politics as usual in Washington, and should continue working to make sure our lawmakers stay clean.

Chapter Three

The Smuggling Gap

"It's not personal, Sonny. It's strictly business."
—Michael Corleone, *The Godfather*

The story of Lai Changxing is a classic rags-to-riches tale
of success in the exuberant capitalism of modern China. The
son of illiterate, penniless farmers, Mr. Lai, along with
countless others, sought his fortune in the Fujian provincial
capital of Xiamen. He arrived in the mid-1980s, just as the
Chinese government was beginning to loosen its chokehold
on private enterprise. Mr. Lai came with no money and no
connections, unable to read and write. By 1990 he was a mil-
lionaire. By 1999 he was a billionaire. He had a finger in all
of Fujian's economic pies, from sports teams to hotels to
shipping. His towering presence in Xiamen's economic life
was such that locals joked of renaming the city "Yuanhua,"
after his holding company.

Today, Mr. Lai's Horatio Alger story has unraveled.
Where he was once known for lavish parties at the "Red

Mansion" he built to entertain business associates, he now lives under house arrest in Vancouver, Canada. He continues to fight extradition to China, where he faces charges of smuggling over $6 billion of merchandise into China from Hong Kong, making him perhaps the greatest smuggler in modern history. Lai Changxing was a shrewd and successful businessman, but one who unfortunately applied his commercial talents to smuggling rather than legal pursuits. Yet learning from Mr. Lai's rational approach to international trade can help us better understand the mindset and methods of economic gangsters—and how to fight them.

Everything Has a Price

Life's decisions involve trading off costs and benefits. That's what economists mean when we say that everything has a price. Price is just the cost side of the cost-benefit ledger. If I buy an apple at the supermarket for a dollar, that's a dollar I can no longer use to buy an orange. Other more elaborate decisions also involve trading off costs and benefits. If I rob a bank, I weigh the benefit of having sacks of hundred dollar bills to spend against the cost of having the police chasing after me and maybe ending up behind bars.

If the supermarket doubles the price of apples, some consumers will switch to buying oranges (or pears). Similarly, if we raise the "price" of a bank holdup by increasing the number of agents working in the FBI's armed robbery unit, we'd expect the number of heists to fall as would-be bank robbers choose to steal cars or break into homes instead (or perhaps give up their criminal ways altogether).

That's the theory at least.[1] In practice we need to understand which costs affect people's decisions, and how. Maybe hiring more G-men doesn't really change the price of bank robbery because your average hood isn't quite as rational (or clever) as Al Capone or Lai Changxing and short-sightedly continues to rob banks despite the higher price. Understanding which costs matter is not an exercise for the armchair economist. Rather than engaging in abstract theorizing and speculation, we need to figure out how to measure the scale of illicit activity and then see how it responds to economic carrots and sticks out in the real world of smugglers and gangsters.

Smuggling as a business

A few decades ago, electronics goods and cheap toys from Asia famously came with a "Made in Hong Kong" stamp on the bottom. These days it's "Made in China." Today, Hong Kong's seven million citizens are too rich to compete in low-wage manufacturing with the factories employing many of the 1.3 billion people just to their north. Hong Kong has returned to its shipping roots and is known primarily as a trading station for the exports China sends all over the world, and for the ever-increasing flow of imports that feed the roaring Chinese economy.

Hong Kong enjoys an especially happy symbiosis with the southern provinces of Guangdong and Fujian, the export engines behind China's growth miracle. Hong Kong provides their manufacturing firms access to one of the most efficient deep-water ports on the planet. In return Hong Kong reaps a steady increase in business from the world's fastest growing economy. Nearly $700 billion worth of goods flows through Hong Kong's larger-than-life port each year.

The staggering scale of Hong Kong's trade—and the

economic dynamism of southern China that it has enabled—
is a direct consequence of the revolution in shipping containerization that has transformed global trade. Loading and
unloading cargo is no longer the domain of burly longshore-
men lifting huge sacks, barrels, or odd-sized pieces of furni-
ture. Nowadays the job has devolved to massive 200-foot
cranes that hoist standardized 40-foot-long containers directly from ship to truck (or railcar), and vice versa.[2] These
cost-cutting innovations are a boon for legitimate exporters
and importers, like the thousands of toy, clothing, and dog
food manufacturers in southern China.

Yet it's easy to imagine how China's Al Capones—the
smugglers of weapons, narcotics, and other contraband—have
also benefited. Inspection technology hasn't kept up with innovations in shipping speed. Most inspections are still done
the old-fashioned way, by eye-balling containers' goods. And
with nearly *24 million* 40-foot containers passing through
Hong Kong in 2006 alone—more than 2,700 every hour—
customs agents can examine the contents of only a tiny fraction of shipments before sending them on their way. No one
really knows what's passing through Hong Kong in those
millions of uniform, anonymous containers.

Perhaps no one profited more handsomely from this
technological mismatch between express shipping and low-
tech inspections than Lai Changxing. Though his racket
was in smuggling, the goods he trafficked were not typically
illegal in and of themselves. In the 1990s, Mr. Lai's import-
export business brought tobacco, gasoline, luxury automobiles, televisions, and other high tariff items into China.
Here's the catch: he imported these goods without paying
the official duties. His business plan was more mundane
than trafficking heroin or weapons-grade plutonium, but

what it lacked in cachet it made up for in profits. According to the 1998 Chinese government investigation that finally brought down Lai's empire, the smuggler had brought $6 billion worth of goods into China from Hong Kong, costing the Chinese government billions in unpaid tariff revenues.

Amidst the millions of shipments passing through customs from Hong Kong into China, it's easy to see how Lai might have gotten away with underreporting the duties he owed. Is that high-tariff tobacco in those containers? No, just some old wood pulp. Some shipments were not reported at all. And how did he get away with this racket for so many years? Corruption: seemingly half the customs officials in China were on his payroll.

Was Lai the tip of a Chinese smuggling iceberg, or was he a lone wolf among otherwise law-abiding importers? We now know a lot about this one man's smuggling empire thanks to the 1998 legal crackdown that tried to bring him to justice. But it's a lot harder to uncover information on the operations of the many other smugglers who never got caught. Beyond Lai, how much smuggling was there, and what means did smugglers employ to secret their goods into China?

It turns out that the answers to these questions are hidden in plain sight. Publicly available trade statistics for China and Hong Kong tell all, if you know where and how to look. While the Chinese government is far more capable of catching and apprehending individual smugglers than economics professors like us, we'll be able to provide a general account of the extent and methods of Chinese smuggling using only these trade statistics—combined with a little economics common sense. Understanding the nature of smuggling is a first step in figuring out how governments can control the Lai Changxing's of the world.

Tariffs and Smugglers' Incentives

You don't have to be a big-time crime boss to understand the economics of smuggling. Just think back to your last vacation abroad. Travelers returning to the United States can bring up to $800 of foreign goods into the country duty-free. After that, Uncle Sam will charge a tax on your purchases. Suppose you bought a $2,000 Gucci handbag in Italy and want to avoid the 10 percent duty (an extra charge of $200) that you'd have to pay if you declared the purchase. You have a couple of options as you nervously shuffle toward the green or red signs at customs. You could pull off the price tag and pretend that it's only a $799 handbag. You could claim you bought it on an earlier trip to Italy. Or you could bury it at the bottom of your suitcase and hope that you won't be pulled aside for a random luggage inspection.

Some obvious factors affect this cost-benefit decision. The main benefit of trying to sneak the handbag through customs is the $200 saved by misreporting. As the tariff rate rises, walking under the green "nothing to declare" arrow will look more and more tempting. On the cost side, the likelihood you get pulled out of line and the scale of punishment both matter. Do you risk a small fine for misreporting—or prison time? Does the Department of Homeland Security randomly check one traveler in ten (pretty risky), or only one in a thousand? (And how random are those random checks anyhow? Did that Pakistan visa from another recent trip land you on the DHS's watch list?) Your method of evading the handbag tariff may also depend on what you're trying to smuggle in. Does the handbag already look fashionably worn, and hence easier to pass off as two years old? Is it small enough to fit discreetly at the bottom of your suitcase?

An importer who treats smuggling as a business decision goes through exactly this type of calculated gamble each day in deciding what to report to the authorities.

How can we see smuggling that the authorities can't? We aren't going to pull out our crowbars and start rummaging through shipments in the ports of Hong Kong or Newark, New Jersey, to find out how many Gucci bags are coming in illegally. Instead, we'll take advantage of some peculiarities in international trade data to get closer to an honest estimate of smuggling.

The way we do it is by comparing how much exporters report sending out of country A into country B, and compare these numbers to what's reported entering country B coming from country A. The difference between these two numbers—the reported value of export shipments versus reported imports—is our measure of smuggling.

The reason this works is because in most countries, including the United States, you can export as much as you like of consumer goods and there's no tariff charge. With the exception of certain sensitive military technologies, the government is happy that someone's buying its products and thus generating livelihoods for its citizens. When you're asked at the airport in Rome what you're taking on the plane with you, there's no downside to telling the truth about your Gucci bag. You can just report honestly that you're bringing a brand new $2,000 handbag on board. However, when you go through customs in New York, you might answer that you bought a cheap handbag or no handbag at all to avoid high import duties. This kind of behavior will leave a funny inconsistency in the official Italy-U.S. trade statistics for handbags: lots of fancy leather items leave Italy on flights to America but few arrive.[3] The more travelers who sneak in undeclared Gucci handbags, the bigger this "smuggling gap" in the official trade statistics will be.

Lai Changxing left gaping holes of this sort in the Hong Kong-China trade numbers. Many containers full of cigarettes and automobiles left Hong Kong headed to the mainland but never arrived, at least according to Chinese import statistics. The same is true of many other businesses operating out of Hong Kong. We'll use this smuggling gap measure of illicit activities to estimate how much Hong Kong exporters are cheating on their tariff payments to the Chinese government. In the absence of widespread smuggling, we should find that what is reported *leaving* Hong Kong destined for China is identical to what is reported as *arriving* in China from Hong Kong. But we find that many Chinese imports—like lots of Lai's products—go missing in action.

Uncovering Smugglers the Economist's Way

The United Kingdom controlled Hong Kong until 1997 through a ninety-nine year lease signed with the Chinese government. While Hong Kong has reverted to Chinese political rule for over a decade now, it continues to enjoy a high degree of economic autonomy as a free trade zone separate from the rest of China. Goods made in Hong Kong are issued tariffs when they enter China. How much needs to be paid at customs depends a lot on what is being imported, and the tariff schedule varies in seemingly inexplicable ways. Chinese trade barriers are a patchwork of highs and lows, resulting from decades of Five Year Plans that directed and controlled the mainland economy.

To shield virtuous Chinese peasants from foreign decadence, for instance, perfume tariffs were set at 55 percent in 1996; for tobacco products, it was 70 percent. Tariffs were also supposed to protect and nurture China's nascent manufacturing and technology sectors. Foreign cars faced tariffs of at least 100 percent, and video monitors 50 percent. Key inputs into the Chinese economic machine, like raw iron and aluminum ores, came in tariff-free, lest the tariffs make Chinese factories uncompetitive. In their great wisdom, Chinese policymakers tinkered in a fine-grained manner with the tariff rates of seemingly very similar products. The tariff on a "boring/milling machine"? That depends on whether it's a "boring/milling machine—numerically controlled" (10 percent) or a "boring/milling machine—other" (20 percent), a difference that persisted through the 1990s.[4] Why the difference? Perhaps the authors of the 1985 Five Year Plan saw an important role for numerically controlled boring machines in the Chinese economy; perhaps the numerically controlled boring machine lobby in China was particularly well organized; or maybe there's no good reason at all. Seemingly arbitrary tariff differences like this show up with remarkable frequency in China, the United States, and many other countries.

This creates a different set of economic incentives for importers of perfume versus importers of iron ore, as well as importers of numerically controlled boring machines versus other boring machines. As a result, perfume makers should smuggle the most and iron ore producers not at all. In general, the higher the tariff rate, the more smuggling will take place to avoid duties, and this should be reflected in a higher smuggling gap in the official Hong Kong-China trade statistics.

Together with coauthor Shang-Jin Wei, this is exactly what we found in the data: there is indeed a much larger smuggling gap in the Hong Kong-China statistics for high-tariff goods, based on trade data for 1996–98.[5] What's remarkable is not only that this relationship exists, but how strong it is. For every 1 percentage point increase in the tariff rate, the smuggling gap rises by 3 percentage points. So the rate of smuggling would be about 30 percent higher for other boring machines (with their 20 percent tariff rate) than for numerically controlled boring machines (10 percent tariff).

This is a large effect, particularly given the high tariff rates that Chinese importers faced until very recently. In fact the extent of smuggling implies that Chinese tariffs were perplexingly high. Imagine what would happen if the government had doubled the tariff rate on other boring machines from 20 to 40 percent. Tariff revenues would double on each boring machine entering the country. However, our calculations suggest that smuggling would increase by roughly 60 percent (by 3 percentage points for each percentage point increase in the tariff). Therefore, fewer than half as many boring machines would now be reported entering the country. The net effect of the tariff increase—double the revenue *per machine* but fewer than half as many machines reported—would be negative. In other words, by jacking up the tariff rate a lot, the government actually earns less money because of the growing number of exporters that now smuggle their way in.[6]

Any increase above a tariff rate of about 30 percent similarly results in lower tariff revenues from smuggling losses. Why then did nearly half of all imported products face tariffs above this level back in the 1990s, if the government was only cheating itself of revenue by setting rates so high?

A couple of explanations come to mind. First, the innocent one. The Chinese government may have been legitimately protecting infant auto or computing (or boring machine) industries, nurturing them behind tariff walls, regardless of the short-run losses in revenue. Eventually, the growth of these industries could yield much greater revenue and national income, at least in theory. Similarly, the government may have been paternalistically setting high tariff barriers on some goods to protect its citizens from the temptations of Chanel perfume and Absolut vodka. Again, the government's objective in that case isn't just collecting tariff revenues. Rather, they wish to protect Chinese culture from outside competition.

A less honorable explanation is that tariff rates were kept high by corrupt government officials precisely *because* it forced importers to find a way around them. On the one hand, smugglers could simply try to deceive port officials about the contents of their shipping containers and hope for the best. But why chance getting caught, and risk one's fate in a Chinese court system where large-scale smuggling sentences range from ten years in a labor camp to the death penalty? It's much safer to buy off the appropriate Chinese government officials by cutting them in on a share of your smuggling profits. Customs officials around the world, in turn, find that they can make a fine living by turning a blind eye to smuggling (for a fee), and thus do their best to keep tariff rates at a high enough level to keep their "services" in high demand.

We have no way of determining exactly how much smuggling occurred despite scrupulous customs officials—or because of the corrupt ones. However, the central government's crackdown on smugglers in the late 1990s suggests that a significant fraction of the illegal trade we've documented took place with the blessing of some Chinese officials. The notorious Lai Changxing had much of the Fujian provincial government on his payroll. Local port officials notified his captains in advance of exactly which containers in a shipment would be singled out for inspection. Those would be filled with the appropriate goods (and duties paid), while hundreds of other containers around them held high-tariff contraband. Sometimes Lai just bought his way around nosey port inspectors entirely. His connections extended to the highest levels of government, including the vice-mayor and head of customs in the port city of Xiamen, and the vice-minister of public security in Beijing.[7]

The Smuggling of Art, and the Art of Smuggling

The village of Monteleone di Spoleto, Italy would like its Etruscan chariot back. Dug up long ago by a local farmer, he reportedly sold the chariot to two Frenchmen in 1902 for a couple of cows. The chariot eventually found its way into the hands of New York's Metropolitan Museum, which has no plans to ship it back to Italy anytime soon. According to the villagers, the chariot was looted under murky, probably illegal circumstances. The museum denies any wrongdoing and dismisses the possibility that they violated American law.[8] Both sides may be right.

Most countries ban or severely restrict the export of antique art and other cultural property. This includes big-time antiquities like Etruscan chariots and Greek statues that would fetch millions, but also cov-

---

ers hundred-dollar trinkets like pre-Columbian pottery shards and nineteenth-century coins. Such objects can only be exported with special government permission, which is rarely forthcoming. Alternatively, rather than suffering through the bureaucratic nightmare of filing for export permits, you could take your chances and pay off a customs agent at the border.

Either way, you're probably free to bring your coins, pottery, statues, and chariots into America. The Department of Homeland Security itself explains in its handbook for art importers that violating a foreign country's law doesn't necessarily mean you're in violation of U.S. law.[9] While it's okay to bring illegally exported items into the country, you *do* have to be honest about what you report to the U.S. authorities. Otherwise, antiquities importers would be guilty of perjury and their merchandise subject to seizure.

Lie about your exports, honestly report your imports. This is starting to sound a lot like our Chinese tariff evaders—only in reverse. Given the incentives art dealers face, it may come as no surprise that a lot more antiques arrive in America each year than the rest of the world sends to the United States. At least that's what the official trade statistics say.[10] The same is true for the art import markets in Switzerland and Germany.

This antique smuggling gap is widest for those countries where it's easiest to bribe your way around export restrictions—Nigeria, Russia, and Syria to name a few. These countries that also get rated as highly corrupt year after year in Transparency International's global rankings. So by providing an honest (or less dishonest) account when their goods arrive in America, antiques smugglers leave fingerprints in the data that are visible to economic detectives.

Eventually, we may be able to use a similar approach to expose arms traders, drug traffickers, and other participants in the darkest corners of international trade. All that's needed is legal differences across countries and a bunch of calculating smugglers who respond to these differences like the textbook economic agents they are.

Bribery: Grease or Sand in the Wheels of Commerce?

This gets us back to the issue we raised in chapter 2 of when and how corruption is bad for the economy. Chinese producers need cheap oil to keep factories running and cars on the road. Mr. Lai was a local hero in Xiamen, credited with keeping prices affordable for the city's poor and fueling rapid economic expansion—albeit at the expense of government tax revenues. In the wake of the government's 1998 smuggling crackdown, official imports into Guangdong province jumped by 10 percent as smuggling declined. But exports plummeted 12 percent as the province's factories struggled to deal with higher-priced imported inputs, like oil and raw materials, which could no longer be smuggled in tariff-free.

The view that smuggling was good for the Chinese economy is the classic "grease the wheels" argument that favors corruption as a way of getting things done in a system burdened by unwieldy bureaucracy and excessive red tape. For an extreme case, in the central African country of Chad it takes two and a half months to deal with the legal paperwork needed to start a business (versus six days in the United States), and acquiring the licenses required to build a warehouse takes nearly half a year (versus a little over a month in the United States).[11] If you have a good business opportunity in Chad, then maybe it's just as well that Chad is also a very corrupt country. At least that way you can probably buy your way around some of the paperwork and delays.

One problem with the view that corruption speeds commerce is that paying bribes to reduce red tape is only half the story. Suppose that companies are willing to pay bribes to do an end run around the rules. Then government officials on the receiving end of these bribes will realize that they can make even *more* money by raising tariffs further, or throwing ever more regulatory barriers in companies' paths. In many countries, like China, the rule enforcers are the rule makers as well, so they may start creating onerous new laws for the sole purpose of extracting larger bribe payments. Companies' willingness to pay bribes helps *cause* the red tape in the first place.

Smuggling Thanksgiving Dinner

There's more than one way to stiff the Chinese government on tariff payments. Suppose, for example, Lai Changxing wanted to bring in a shipment of one thousand ten-yuan frozen chickens, and wants to find a way around paying the 20 percent chicken tariff. First, Mr. Lai could lie about the value of his chickens, claiming that his ten-yuan chickens are worth only five yuan apiece. But this could get Mr. Lai and his frozen chickens in some hot water if they run across a customs agent who knows something about poultry. Alternatively, he could claim that his shipping container has only five-hundred chickens rather than a thousand. But this, too, is risky business if a customs agent opens up the container and starts counting his chickens. Even if border officials never peek into Mr. Lai's chicken shipment, they may know how much an average chicken weighs and find the five-hundred chickens in the shipment to be suspiciously heavy (containers are routinely weighed for safety reasons).

Finally, Mr. Lai could reduce his tariff bill by claiming that his chickens aren't chickens at all, but some other bird with a lower tariff rate. For example, if turkeys imported into China face only a 10 percent tariff, then Mr. Lai could cut his tariff payments in half by claiming that his shipment of frozen poultry parts is actually turkey meat. This will be somewhat easier to get away with at customs than claiming the poultry shipment is, say, four-door sedans: chickens and turkeys weigh similar amounts and require similar care in shipping. If an honest customs agent happens to peek inside, he may well mistake turkeys for chickens but is unlikely to confuse chickens with a midsize automobile.

As we've already discovered, there is a large smuggling gap in the *value* of shipments reported by Hong Kong and Chinese customs officials in their official trade statistics: the value of high-tariff chicken shipments entering China is less than the value of chicken shipments leaving Hong Kong. To figure out whether this is because of disappearing chickens or underpriced chickens, we can also examine the smuggling gaps in the *quantity* of imports, something that importers also have to report in the official statistics. If the smuggling quantity gap is greater for higher-tariff goods, then importers must be lying about the number of products they're bringing in (reporting five hundred rather than one thousand chickens). If the smuggling gap in shipment quantity is no different for high-tariff versus low-tariff goods, then the difference in shipment value that we've observed is because importers are lying about the price of each item, so shipment value is lower on arrival in China not because there are fewer chickens, but because the chickens are reported as being worth five-yuan rather than ten-yuan each. Then there is the third possibility of calling chickens turkeys, which we'll return to shortly.

In the official Hong Kong and China trade data, we find that importers stay honest on the number of chickens and other merchandise but lie a lot about the value of each individual item. This isn't surprising. It may be difficult to verify the final market price of particular poultry parts (are they plump or scrawny birds? organic? free-range?), but it's easy to weigh forty-foot containers and use this information to calculate how much is in each shipment.

Figuring out whether high-tariff chickens turn into low-tariff turkeys is trickier. Think about the smuggling gap for the 10 percent tariff turkeys that are very similar in appearance to 20 percent tariff chickens. If importers mislabel these higher-tariff chickens as turkeys, then we should observe more turkeys entering China from Hong Kong (in the Chinese data) than left Hong Kong destined for China (in the Hong Kong stats). That is, we should observe a *negative* smuggling gap for turkeys. And if the tariff on chickens goes up further to 30 percent (or if the tariff on turkeys drops to 0 percent), we'd expect an even greater number of "turkeys" coming into China compared to chickens. In general, we'd expect that if the tariff rate rises on goods that are similar to turkeys (other types of poultry—chickens, ducks, quail), the number of reported turkeys will increase, so that the turkey smuggling gap becomes more and more negative. But the smuggling gap on four-dour sedans and other products that'll never be mistaken for poultry will be unaffected by tariff changes on poultry.

The trade data tells us that this chicken-to-turkey sleight of hand actually accounts for *most* of the disappearing chickens, and in fact most of the overall Hong Kong–China smuggling gap in general. If you were to take the Hong Kong export and Chinese import numbers at face value, you would believe that there was a magical transformation from chickens to turkeys at the border crossings from Hong Kong into China. And similarly, other boring machines mysteriously become numerically controlled boring machines. In fact, it's just the paper trail left behind by smugglers reacting to high Chinese tariff rates by mislabeling their shipments.

Let Chickens be Chickens: How to Turn Economic Incentives against Smugglers

Beyond keeping academic economists like ourselves gainfully employed, the search for Hong Kong's disappearing chickens can also help the Chinese government realign importers' incentives away from smuggling.

We don't have to speculate on the Chinese government's preferred methods for putting Hong Kong smugglers out of business. In the 1998 anticorruption campaign that sent Lai Changxing fleeing from China for fear of his life, many others—the smugglers themselves, as well as the high-level Chinese government officials that served as their accomplices—were caught and punished. Hundreds received long prison sentences and a few dozen the death penalty.

In addition to the severe penalties, better government customs enforcement ensured that the chances of smugglers getting caught increased. Outside investigators were brought down to Guangdong and Fujian from the capital to clean up the customs houses, and they opened up and searched many more shipping containers on arrival.

The government's new approach centered squarely on increasing the risks of smuggling rather than reducing its benefits. But this anticorruption drive came at a very high cost itself. We have already mentioned that prices for industrial inputs shot up following the 1998 campaign, as Chinese businesses had to pay prices that factored in extra tariff costs. The enforcement efforts themselves were also a burden to both government public finances and Chinese manufacturers: long transport delays became routine as customs agents scrambled for the time and resources to scrutinize the larger volume of shipments flagged for inspection.

Some smugglers were surely dissuaded from continuing in their chosen line of work, but they did not disappear entirely despite the stepped-up enforcement. They merely adopted new approaches to elude the new measures, albeit less cost effectively than before. In 2006, authorities uncovered an underground tunnel connecting Hong Kong to its Chinese sister city of Shenzhen via the cities' sewer pipes, through which high-tariff computer chips and mobile phones were being surreptitiously trafficked into China. Others brought small shipments of televisions and computers across on speedboats in the dead of night. Other traders stuck to the ports but sent the contraband in small enough quantities to ensure that, if caught by the authorities, they would escape the most severe legal punishments. But by transporting goods in secret tunnels and midnight runs and small batches, Hong Kong's smugglers were losing out on the containerization revolution that makes international trade so lucrative to begin with.

Were the Chinese government's antismuggling efforts worth it in the end? It's hard to say. Obviously, the government was effective at punishing some corrupt officials, but it may have been equally effective in reducing local economic growth, at least in the short run, as the cost of imported inputs rose. We think that a different approach, focusing more on reducing smuggling's benefits rather than its costs, would have been equally effective but at a far lower cost. Most of the smuggling we uncovered didn't involve underreporting on price or quantity. Rather, it was the "chickens-turned-turkeys" that accounted for most of the smuggling gap—smugglers simply lied about the types of products they were bringing into the country. So a good start would be to set turkey tariffs equal to chicken tariffs, and in general equate tariffs of all goods that are similar enough to be mislabeled. Tariffs don't need to be reduced to zero: governments *do* need to raise tax revenue somehow and it's useful to collect some of it through tariffs. And the tariff on chickens can in fact be different from the tariff on cars, as long as it's not too far different from the turkeys that can easily masquerade as chickens. The bottom line is that similar products should have similar tariffs to avoid the chicken-turkey problem.

Reducing tariff dispersion would only be a first step in the cat-and-mouse game between smugglers and enforcers. For every government action, there will be a reaction. Mislabeling was the lowest cost approach to evading tariffs under the old pre-1998 customs system, but we've already seen that Chinese smugglers are resourceful in finding other ways around customs laws. This reaction may involve a shift to the other channels that we have already discussed—underreporting quantities or values, or perhaps bypassing the ports altogether by docking and off-loading goods in remote locations. Or they may cook up something else entirely that neither we nor the Chinese government has even thought of. But by plugging up the easiest channels for tariff evasion, the Chinese government would be forcing a reaction that makes smuggling less profitable and begins to chip away at this gritty underside of economic globalization.

Coming to America

The United States, like China, has a hodgepodge of tariff levels resulting from a mix of government bureaucracy, inertia, and a hefty dose of industry lobbying. The steel market serves as a model of this tariff jumble. In 2001, the *Wall Street Journal* reported on a "steady, lucrative . . . business in smuggling" in the steel industry.[12] American importers were taking advantage of wide tariff dispersion in nearly identical steel products, with rates ranging from pennies to hundreds of dollars per ton. Low-grade wire rod (10 percent tariff) came in reported as high-grade rod (no tariff), steel bars became rolled steel, and so on. President George W. Bush famously tried to increase steel tariffs by 8 to 30 percent in 2002 to save an ailing industry based in the politically important swing state of Pennsylvania. America's European and Asian trading partners sounded a chorus of disapproval and threatened retaliation (including tariffs on orange juice targeting the political swing state of Florida), and in the end Bush backed down. By December 2003, most tariffs on steel had dropped to zero, and steel imports reported in official data immediately shot up, mostly due to a jump in legal shipments but at least in part because U.S. importers no longer had to think like smugglers.

The steel tariff debate was resolved in a manner that will reduce smuggling and law breaking, but the U.S. tariff schedule remains chockablock with peculiar inconsistencies that, according to the *New York Times*, are "a vestige of smoke-filled, backroom trade negotiations."[13] What's the tariff on woolen shirts? Believe it or not, it depends on whether you're a man or a woman: it's 18 percent on men's shirts, more than double the rate for women's. It isn't that the government discriminates against men alone. If you're in the market for a bathing suit, the rate for women at 27.8 percent is one-and-a-half times the tariff on men's swimwear. While we haven't studied the U.S. apparel import and export data in as much detail as that of Chinese statistics, we'll guess that many woolen shirts, bathing suits, and other clothing just may be getting sex changes as they cross the border into America. The best way of ending this peculiar practice will be to create gender equity in tariff rates.

Before leaving Chinese smugglers for the U.N. diplomats we'll meet in the next chapter, it's worth reemphasizing that in China as well as the United States, laws usually get written for a reason. There are often high tariffs and tariff differences between men's and women's clothes because someone benefits from the arrangement. Maybe domestic producers of women's bathing suits have an exceptionally strong lobby and have convinced their congresspeople to erect protectionist barriers on bikinis, or maybe customs officials in Shenzhen can earn a little extra cash by looking the other way on mislabeled chicken imports. Simple changes that make economic sense may remain elusive because they interfere with the livelihoods of big business, or corrupt customs agents and other law enforcement officials.

This is precisely where reforms so often get stalled. Yet how can we get the government or the public at large to rally around antismuggling efforts, or anticorruption programs in general? While we economists refer to ourselves as social scientists, we have traditionally had less to say about the "social" side of behavior. How do people form their ideologies, attitudes, tastes, and beliefs? Why are bribery and lawbreaking a matter of disgrace in some countries, and simply the norm in others? And how can reformers transform people's values and attitudes to create pressure for social change? While this has traditionally been the intellectual domain of sociologists and psychologists, it's central to corruption reform, and in the next chapter we economists will have our say.

Chapter Four

Nature or Nurture? Understanding the Culture of Corruption

The Curious Case of Dr. Antanas Mockus

In October 1994, Antanas Mockus, a professor of philosophy and mathematics, was elected mayor of Bogotá, Colombia, by a landslide. Bogotá was still reeling from the legacy of Pablo Escobar and the drug wars of the previous decade. Crime was rampant—the city held the dubious distinction of being the murder capital of the world, with over 4,200 homicides in 1993 alone—and the municipal government was notoriously corrupt. Bogotanos were fed up and Mockus, an "anti-politician" by his own account, who had never held public office, was charged with the seemingly impossible task of creating order amidst chaos.

Once in office, Mayor Mockus quickly sprang into action, stationing mimes at the city's busiest intersections. Yes, *mimes*. His vision for taming the lawbreaking drug lords of Colombia included the hiring of a group of theater students wearing white face paint and tights to help to enforce traffic rules. The mimes didn't carry guns, nor could they issue tickets. They laid down the law using methods—mimicry and ridicule—that are traditional to the vocation of the mime, but not usually associated with policing (or at least good policing).

Mimes attached themselves to jaywalkers, striding behind them and mocking their every move. Reckless drivers were targeted with similar methods. Mimes carried an arsenal of cards with a thumbs-down printed on them to flash, soccer-referee-style, to drivers blocking intersections or running red lights. This quickly became participatory street theater, as the mimes gave out thumbs-down cards to civilians eager to lend a hand. In a matter of months, the fraction of pedestrians obeying traffic signals reportedly jumped from 26 percent to 75 percent. Indeed, these mime-based interventions proved so popular and effective in reforming behavior that Mockus hired four hundred more mimes to extend the long arm of mimicry to the rest of the city.[1]

Mockus's reform agenda started small but soon went well beyond traffic compliance, as he instituted a broader range of measures to tackle the city's violence, crime, and poverty head-on. He introduced a gun buyback program that offered cash compensation and legal amnesty to get illegal firearms off the streets; he closed down the transit police department, whose 2,000 members were notorious bribe-takers; and he initiated large-scale public works to bring basic services to the city's poor, including massive investments in public transit. But Mockus felt that efforts at attitudinal change were fundamental to all of his reforms, and that transforming civic culture was the key to solving his city's myriad ills.[2]

Mockus's efforts have in fact transformed the city of Bogotá. After stepping down in 1997 to make a run for president of Colombia, Mockus came back for a second highly successful term in 2001. By the time he left office in 2004, Bogotá's murder rate, while still high by U.S. standards, had fallen by 70 percent, and kidnappings had declined even more steeply. Bogotá's crime rates are now among the lowest of any large Latin American city. The Bogotá municipal budget runs surpluses rather than deficits and still finds the money to build more schools, libraries, roads, and parks—and even public art installations. Most striking, however, is the change among Bogotá's residents, who have genuine pride in the city's sudden renaissance.

If these culture-based reforms sound a little strange to you, imagine how bizarre they must seem to us—a pair of economists inculcated in the mantra that "incentives matter," a view that was so successful in explaining smuggling patterns in the South China trade (in chapter 3). Clearly, some of Mockus's policies are in keeping with economics' emphasis on the role of incentives: give me your gun and I will give you 130,000 pesos in return (not quite as dramatic as it sounds given an exchange rate of 1,300 pesos to the dollar, but still real money). But what of the mime-based policing of Bogotá's drivers, where the only consequence of bad behavior was exposure to public ridicule?

Only a very narrow-minded economist could think that tangible rewards or punishments alone drive behavior. People surely do respond to direct economic incentives, but they may also respond to the fuzzier incentives that come from social sanction or one's own conscience. Just think back to how you felt the last time you dropped a gum wrapper on the sidewalk, or some other act that, while perhaps not illegal, brought glares of disapproval from passersby. Mimes can't collect fines or toss scofflaws in jail, but the fear of ridicule may very well have helped transform Bogotá's rude drivers and pedestrians into more orderly citizens.

The story of Dr. Antanas Mockus reads like a bedtime fairytale for social reformers. Mockus was successful because he mixed psychology and showmanship with traditional incentives in many of his reform efforts. For example, when Bogotá faced a municipal water shortage, the new mayor appeared showering (and half-naked) on television, turning off the water as he lathered, and encouraging others to do the same. But meanwhile, his government also flogged the point that households could save money by reducing water consumption. It's thus hard to say whether Mockus's ingenious attempts at changing social norms were central to the city's rebirth, or whether he was simply an honest, effective leader, well-endowed with charisma who knew how to add a spoonful of sugar to make the traditional medicine go down.

It's Not Just the Economy, Stupid

Moving beyond the curious case of one unusual South American mayor, we face the much broader question of why conduct in some societies is dominated by law-abiding behavior while corruption is the norm in others. What keeps New Yorkers or San Franciscans from slipping a twenty-dollar bill to policemen who pull them over for speeding, while such transactions are the norm on the chaotic roads of Lagos and Dhaka—and, for that matter, Palermo, Sicily?

You don't try to pay off street cops in New York because you know that it's likely to buy you a first-hand look at prison conditions on Riker's Island. By contrast, not only can you rightly assume you'll get away with bribing a policeman in Lagos, it's actually expected of you. The policeman's salary is probably little more than twenty dollars a month and he needs the extra cash to feed his family. Indeed, you're probably more likely to get in trouble with the police authorities in Nigeria if you don't pay a bribe than if you do. Similar lessons apply in everyday dealings with providers of public services: in the United States we aren't expected to pay bribes to obtain access to water, phone service, or electricity, as is the case in much of the world.

There's more here than just differences in expectations about the way traffic cops or bureaucrats at the water utility will respond to attempted bribes. In some places, the necessities of daily existence turn ordinary folk into rule-breaking economic gangsters. Even if weak legal enforcement laid the foundation for a system of bribery and corruption, once in place it becomes a matter of habit: after a while everyone knows bribery is simply *the way things get done*. By contrast, most Americans grow up with a very different set of cultural norms, where from a young age parents, teachers, and other authority figures instill the idea that *bribery just isn't right*.

Is corruption simply a matter of weak law enforcement, or do background experiences also affect the decision to behave corruptly? It matters a lot for how we try to stamp out corruption—whether to emphasize the carrots and sticks of economic incentives, or follow Mockus's lead in focusing on culture. But in practice—as Mockus discovered—it's hard to separate the two. In fact, we may really never know whether it was mainly mimes or fines that changed behavior in Bogotá.

And it's also difficult to do this by comparing corruption levels across countries. Once again culture, as well as law enforcement levels, differ from country to country. Suppose, for example, we wanted to resolve the culture versus enforcement question by comparing Nigeria to Norway. Most people would say that Nigeria, which was near the bottom (i.e., worst) in Transparency International's 2005 Corruption Perceptions Index, has both a weak culture of rule compliance and weak legal enforcement. In contrast, Norway, a perennial front-runner for the least corrupt country on earth, has both a strong culture of rule compliance as well as strong legal enforcement.

So comparing Nigerians and Norwegians is a matter of apples and oranges. We must account for both difference in law enforcement *and* culture (as well as other factors) in comparing corruption in these two countries. To understand the role of culture alone, we need to somehow put Norwegians in an environment with weak legal enforcement to find out what Nordic conscience and social norms—and not the Norwegian police—tell them to do.

Norwegians, alas, are not lab rats, and would resist changes in their laws just to satisfy our curiosity about the impact of culture versus incentives in keeping corruption in check. Besides, even if we could move the residents of Oslo to Lagos for the experiment, we would still face the problem of measuring illicit activities (something we've already discussed at some length in earlier chapters).

Ideally, we could organize an event that would bring public officials from all over the world to a safe haven where they faced no legal constraints on behavior, and then have some means of measuring their corrupt behavior. Actually, that isn't as impossible as it first sounds. Indeed, this is (or was) the anarchist fantasyland occupied by diplomats at the United Nations in New York City, who could park their cars wherever and whenever they wanted and never fear the wrath of Manhattan's eagle-eyed meter maids.[3]

Diplomatic Immunity

In the Hollywood blockbuster *Lethal Weapon II*, an "apartheid-vintage" South African diplomat named Arjen Rudd openly runs a major drug smuggling operation out of the country's Los Angeles consulate, protected from federal prosecution by flashing his ID and reciting the phrase "diplomatic immunity" whenever he finds himself in hot water. While there are, at least in theory, limits to diplomatic protection that deter economic gangsters from trafficking narcotics, robbing banks, and generally raising hell, Consul Rudd is nearly correct in telling Mel Gibson's character, the slightly crazed LAPD Sergeant Martin Riggs, "My dear officer, you could not even give me a parking ticket!"

This characterization of parking privileges is slightly off in one important sense: diplomats in New York City and elsewhere *can* in fact be issued tickets for parking illegally. But unlike us common folk, diplomats never have to pay or say they're sorry or live in fear of the tow truck. What on earth, then, would compel a U.N. mission official to pay his/her parking tickets—or for that matter, even bother looking for a legal parking spot in Manhattan, where (legal) room at the curb is nearly as scarce as an affordable apartment?[4] The answer, of course, is because it's the right thing to do, a matter of conscience and culture.

Remarkably then, diplomats at their countries' U.N. missions provide a very close match to the subjects in our hypothetical experiment for distinguishing the effects of legal deterrence and culture on corruption. The thousands of accredited, mid- and upper-level diplomats from nearly every country on earth who congregate in New York City face no formal legal barriers to parking their cars illegally. Recall our definition of corruption from chapter 1: "The illegal use of public office for private gain." How better to describe a U.N. mission official hiding behind diplomatic immunity when double-parking on a crowded street during rush hour?

Since they must all assemble at the United Nations complex in midtown, U.N. diplomats face a very similar set of daily parking travails. By the same token, most (78 percent) U.N. mission offices themselves are located within a half-mile of the U.N. Plaza. So even on the days these officials warm desk chairs or munch canapés in their own offices, they nearly all face the same grim parking problem in the same neighborhood. The decision to take the time to find a legal piece of curb, pay for private parking, or simply take the subway is a matter of moral rather than legal sanction. The benefits of breaking the law are basically the same across nationalities, while the psychological or social cost varies according to an individual diplomat's attitude toward breaking the law, and you can reasonably think of this guilt (or lack thereof) as part of the diplomat's culture. Diplomatic economic gangsters will use their parking privileges to double-park with abandon, while those constrained by conscience will obey the rules.

This also provides us with a chance to watch the handoff of cash, as it were, that we couldn't observe in earlier cases. Here, we are blessed by the peculiar nature of diplomatic immunity in parking. While there can be no prosecution of diplomats, their violations are nonetheless carefully tracked by the city. Thanks to the detailed records provided by the New York City government, we were able to match every unpaid parking violation from November 1997 until November 2005 to the name and country of the violator, as well as the exact time, type, and location of the violation. We can follow the parking careers of each diplomat throughout his or her tenure at the United Nations, providing us a unique database showing which diplomatic missions ignore New York's parking laws, and how often.[5]

There's one more piece to this puzzle. Unfortunately, we do not have information on actual bribes paid or received to generate a measure of home country corruption. So we are forced to rely on the same survey-based corruption measure of which we were somewhat critical in chapter 1 because of the cheap-talk problem. We use an index developed by researchers at the World Bank, who average the results of a number of individual corruption indexes.[6] Each of these indexes reflects the responses of foreign investors, local business owners, and other country experts with insider knowledge on local corruption practices. For example, in one survey investors are asked: "In your industry, how commonly do firms make undocumented extra payments or bribes connected with tax payments?" They are also asked about the bribes government officials expect in order to produce favorable judicial decisions, public utilities services, and to award public contracts. The higher the World Bank index score, the more corrupt these experts think the country is.

With these measures in hand, we may link up country corruption performance to country parking performance—and in the process, answer this chapter's main question: In the absence of legal deterrents, are officials from corrupt countries more likely to break the rules?

Parking through the Eyes of a Diplomat: An Example

Before getting into our cross-country comparison of violations, it is instructive—and also quite entertaining—to examine the checkered history of one Kuwaiti diplomat to
whom we present the Lifetime Achievement Award for New
York City parking violations. The record of parking violations for "Ambassador X" is shown in figure 4.1.

Ambassador X arrived in New York City in April 1999, a
year and a half into our dataset. He quickly set to work making up for lost time, generating 249 violations during the re-
mainder of that calendar year, even though he was apparently
on vacation (and violation-free) for much of August. He
kept up his record pace, accumulating 526 violations in
2000—more than ten per week, or two per work day!—and
351 through August 2001, before easing off that autumn to a
rate of just two per week. We can also follow Ambassador X
on his perambulations about Manhattan.

The first thing to notice is that Ambassador X spends
an awful lot of time hanging around the United Nations.
This should not come as a great surprise—that's where Ambassador X works each day. In fact, if you want to spin a
charitable interpretation of Ambassador X's parking record,
you might say that most of his violations were committed in
the line of duty: he is a model of self-sacrifice for the good of
his country.

But Ambassador X was also something of a roving parking bandit, generating a paper trail of his abuse of parking
privileges throughout the island of Manhattan. So, it seems
likely that some of his unpaid tickets are the result of personal business. Note the string of violations in Greenwich
Village and on the Upper East Side: both neighborhoods are

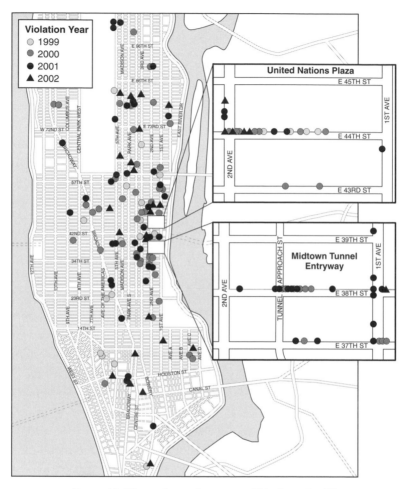

Figure 4.1: The parking adventures of "Ambassador X"

far from the United Nations but do offer some of New York's finest wining and dining.

To an economist, Ambassador X's behavior is hardly surprising. In fact, this is how *all* diplomats should behave according to basic economic theory, as long as New York City cannot punish diplomatic parking violators. Just as no rational person should leave a $20 bill lying on the ground, why should any diplomat leave a perfectly good double-parking spot unoccupied? (At 5 percent, double-parking accounts for its fair share of our total violations. The most common violation, by the way, was parking in a "No Standing—Loading Zone," with 43 percent of infringements, followed by parking in front of a fire hydrant, and overstaying an expired parking meter.)

Turning from bon vivant Kuwaiti Ambassador X to the Norwegian U.N. Mission staff, we catch our first glimpse of Non-Economic Man. Despite New York's inability to punish diplomatic scofflaws, no Norwegian diplomat accumulated a single unpaid parking violation in New York City during our sample period. The same holds for their Nordic neighbors, the Swedes.

The fact that Norwegians and Swedes are inclined to obey the law suggests a link between corruption and culture, but it's hardly proof. Ambassador X does not come from a country with a strong reputation for fighting corruption. But neither is Kuwait seen as one of the world's most corrupt countries, either. Indeed, his country is about average on the World Bank corruption index. The real test is whether there's a general statistical relationship across many countries between parking violations in New York City and the cultural tolerance of corruption back home.

The Truth about Diplomatic Parking Violations

To generate a comparable measure of parking misbehavior in New York City for each country, we simply add up all of the violations committed by each country's diplomats, and divide

Average annual unpaid parking violations per diplomat

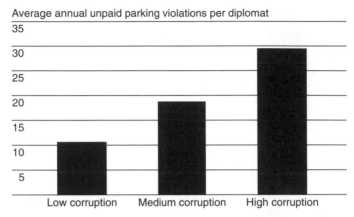

Figure 4.2: Country corruption and unpaid New York City parking violations per diplomat from 11/1997 to 11/2002

by the number of U.N. officials from that country, giving us a "per diplomat" measure of misbehavior. This effectively evens the playing field among big embassies from large countries such as Russia (eighty-six diplomats) and tiny countries like Chad (two diplomats) with a few lonely emissaries.

You can see the relationship between our New York City diplomatic parking violations score (i.e., our measure of corruption "culture") and home-country corruption in graphical form in figure 4.2. We've divided the countries of the world into three groups—high corruption (the top quarter of countries according to the World Bank index), low corruption (the bottom quarter), and medium corruption (everyone in between). The heights of the bar graphs in figure 4.2 tell us how many unpaid parking violations per year were racked up by an average diplomat in each of the three groups. The bar on the left—the diplomats from low corruption countries—reaches a height of a little over ten violations per year on average. The high corruption diplomats in the right-hand bar accumulated nearly three times as many, with nearly thirty unpaid violations each year. And the middling corruption diplomats are somewhere in between. So diplomats from high-corruption countries (the right-hand bar) are flouting New York City parking laws, while those from countries with low corruption largely obey the law, despite the absence of legal consequences.

As another way of understanding this relationship, we list the countries with the most and least violations per diplomat in tables 4.1 and 4.2, along with their World Bank corruption index rankings. The Hall of Shame in table 4.1 includes many countries that also score poorly in the corruption rankings. For example, Egypt, Chad, and Bulgaria are all countries that are part of the right-hand bar in our graph above. The diplomats that abide by parking laws (if not the economic laws of self-interest) in table 4.2 are, for the most part, in the left-hand bar, with very low country-corruption ratings and zero violations.

Many of the countries in table 4.2 won't raise any eyebrows. For instance the Scandinavians perennially rank among the least corrupt in cross-country corruption surveys. Between 1997 and 2005, there were a total of only twelve unpaid violations shared among the sixty-six diplomats from Finland, Norway, Denmark, and Sweden combined—and almost all of these were committed by one bad Finn. But the list of countries where diplomats apparently put honor above self-interest does contain a few surprises. For example, Ecuador and Colombia both have perfectly clean parking slates, despite the experts' view of them as fairly corrupt places. But there is rarely a single, perfect explanation for anything. All sorts of random things aside from home-country corruption presumably influence any individual diplomat's

TABLE 4.1

The Parking Hall of Shame: The 20 Countries with the Highest
Average Unpaid Annual New York City Parking Violations per
Diplomat, from 11/1997 to 11/2002

Rank	Country name	Violations per diplomat	Corruption score
1	KUWAIT	249.4	−1.07
2	EGYPT	141.4	0.25
3	CHAD	125.9	0.84
4	SUDAN	120.6	0.75
5	BULGARIA	119.0	0.50
6	MOZAMBIQUE	112.1	0.77
7	ALBANIA	85.5	0.92
8	ANGOLA	82.7	1.05
9	SENEGAL	80.2	0.45
10	PAKISTAN	70.3	0.76
11	IVORY COAST	68.0	0.35
12	ZAMBIA	61.2	0.56
13	MOROCCO	60.8	0.10
14	ETHIOPIA	60.4	0.25
15	NIGERIA	59.4	1.01
16	SYRIA	53.3	0.58
17	BENIN	50.4	0.76
18	ZIMBABWE	46.2	0.13
19	CAMEROON	44.1	1.11
20	MONTENEGRO & SERBIA	38.5	0.97

decision to park in a loading zone on a particular day, and as a result of this "noise" the statistical relationship between corruption and parking violations (like any other statistical relationship) isn't perfect.

Aside from cases of unexpectedly honest (or dishonest)

TABLE 4.2

The Good Guys: Countries with Zero Unpaid Annual New York
City Parking Violations per Diplomat, from 11/1997 to 11/2002
(among countries with more than 500,000 population
and 5 U.N. mission staff)

Country name	Violations per diplomat	Corruption score
AUSTRALIA	0.0	−2.21
CANADA	0.0	−2.51
COLOMBIA	0.0	0.61
DENMARK	0.0	−2.57
ECUADOR	0.0	0.74
GREECE	0.0	−0.85
IRELAND	0.0	−2.15
ISRAEL	0.0	−1.41
JAMAICA	0.0	0.26
JAPAN	0.0	−1.16
NETHERLANDS	0.0	−2.48
NORWAY	0.0	−2.35
PANAMA	0.0	0.28
SWEDEN	0.0	−2.55
TURKEY	0.0	0.01
UNITED KINGDOM	0.0	−2.33

diplomats, there may also be factors beyond corruption that
systematically predict the number of violations per diplomat.
Most obviously, New York's legal parking spots are extremely
expensive—around $15 if you're stopping by for a half-hour
meeting, or $450 per month. This figure may be just a minor
cost of doing diplomatic business for wealthy Dutch or Japanese
diplomats, but a month of parking in midtown Manhattan

costs twice as much as an average person earns each year in Chad or Sudan. So maybe only diplomats from rich countries (which are also more likely to be countries with effective rule of law) can afford to indulge their consciences, while a poor diplomat from Chad faces the choice between parking illegally and explaining his parking tab to his boss back home.

This rather charitable view of socially deviant parking sounds plausible but doesn't hold up to scrutiny. After all, diplomats lacking the budget to park legally could just take the subway to work like millions of middle-class New Yorkers. We can actually test whether corruption or income better explains parking violations by determining how much of the pattern in figure 4.2 is due to corruption directly, and how much is due to country income. And when we run a "horse race" between these two factors using a statistical approach called multiple regression analysis, it turns out that corruption does a much better job of explaining parking violations than country income.

There are other ways—simpler ones that don't rely on statistical analysis—to figure out whether our results follow from the possibility that only diplomats from rich countries can afford parking garages. We might concede that Chadian diplomats may be forced to double-park near the United Nations during business hours to get their work done. However, it's harder to use the poverty excuse to explain why they park in loading zones at night outside bars in Greenwich Village (following Ambassador X's example), or wreak traffic havoc by double-parking on busy cross-streets during rush hour. Even limiting ourselves to these socially egregious and clearly self-serving violations, we still see the same pattern.

A *Parking Spot You Can't Refuse*

While poor countries dominate the bottom end of both the World Bank corruption index and our measure of parking violations, we quickly start running into rich countries as we make our way up the list. It may not surprise *Godfather* fans—or Italians themselves, for that matter—to find that Italy comes in with the most violations per diplomat in Western Europe. As the birthplace of the Sicilian Mafia, Italy's legacy of political corruption is not simply a matter of gangster film and HBO mythos.

Beyond the recent corruption scandals surrounding prime minister (and media mogul) Silvio Berlusconi, Italy's culture of corruption extends into many other facets of life and society. The national soccer team competed in—and ultimately won—the 2006 World Cup under a cloud of match-fixing allegations involving referee intimidation and payoffs in the Italian soccer league. Alleged misconduct involved officials from four professional clubs of world renown. Despite threats of serious legal penalties (including demotion to the Italian soccer minor leagues and bans from competition for those involved), prosecutors eventually weakened nearly all penalties against the implicated clubs and individuals. So at least for professional soccer players, Italy remains a country bedeviled by a corruption culture as well as ineffectual legal punishment for those who do get caught.

In contrast, Kremlin-watchers may be surprised to see that Russia's diplomatic corps seems inclined to obey New York's parking regulations. In this case, a short history lesson is in order. In the mid-1990s, an echo of Cold War politics was heard on New York City streets. At the time, Russia was the number one parking offender, and tensions rose between the Russians and the New York City government, culminating in a scuffle between a drunken Russian U.N. mission official and a ticket issuer.[7] This is one instance where an injudicious choice of parking spot actually threatened to escalate into an international diplomatic incident, and the then pro-Western Russian government quite sensibly put heavy pressure on its diplomats to behave.

What about the United States?

In light of the recent headlines over congressional corruption rackets and corporate larceny on a grand scale, readers are surely wondering what the behavior of U.S. diplomats has to say about American norms and values. But the United States is absent from our analysis since diplomatic privileges only apply to officials working abroad.

There are other ways, however, to use diplomatic parking habits to gain a view of our national character. One approach is to look at a country that we think is culturally very close to America, and assume that U.S. diplomats would probably behave a lot like theirs. While the Canadians among us (including Ray) may bristle at the notion, Canada is an awful lot like the United States. Canada *is* different, of course, in important ways—including a more generous social safety net, less gun crime, and the province of Quebec.

(Canadians also consume three times as many doughnuts per capita as Americans, but we're not sure that this says much about the integrity of their diplomats.) However, in many ways we are similar. For purposes of comparison, Canada is hard to beat in terms of geography, income levels, democratic political traditions, British colonial heritage, the English language, and popular culture (doughnut consumption notwithstanding). If we believe that American diplomats really would behave like our Dudley-Do-Right neighbors to the north, you can add America to the list of parking saints: Canada's U.N. mission never generated a single scofflaw throughout our study period. Someone in the mission did get a couple of tickets once, but they were promptly paid.

Canadian readers are surely wondering why all this talk of a strong Canadian character of legal compliance in light of the findings of the 2006 inquiry on corruption in Jean Chrétien's Liberal government. We would argue that this episode only reinforces our main point: not only did shady government deals come to light quickly (suggesting that Canada has effective civil institutions for catching this sort of thing), the scandal generated public outrage that helped to topple the Liberals. Corrupt Canadian officials are usually held accountable; corrupt Italians are not.

One might make similar claims for the Jack Abramoff influence-peddling scandal in the U.S. Congress, or the creative accounting at Enron, for that matter. In fact, in the 2006 mid-term Congressional elections, a broad public backlash was already in evidence, as voters listed corruption and influence-peddling in government as one of their primary concerns. The fact that these abuses were discovered and justice was served is evidence of a healthy set of national norms and legal institutions.

CHAPTER FOUR

Because diplomatic privileges are only relevant outside of the home country, the other way to collect evidence is to see how U.S. diplomats behave abroad. But here, one recent example is not so reassuring. Since 2003, London has levied a modest "congestion charge" on vehicles driving into the central business district. The idea is to pare traffic and boost use of public transportation. Under the Geneva Conventions governing diplomatic immunity that also gave us our parking tickets data, diplomats are not obliged to pay this charge, but most diplomats in London do so, nonetheless. One major exception is the U.S. diplomatic corps, which has the dubious honor of accumulating the greatest number of outstanding fines for nonpayment of the congestion charge—a cumulative total far exceeding $1 million since 2003.

And which countries are the United States's peers in the game of dodging the congestion charge? Nigeria, Angola, and Sudan—all high-corruption countries that fall in the top fifteen in New York City parking tickets. U.S. diplomats do even worse than the Kuwaitis in London. Perhaps Canada is not the right comparison country after all . . .

Sticking It to Uncle Sam at the Parking Meter

The fact that diplomats from so many countries—and particularly those with low-corruption governments—garner so few parking tickets in New York flies in the face of standard economic assumptions. Clearly, emotions, norms, and psychology do govern a lot of what we do.[8] We were already venturing into the domain of psychology when we talked before about social norms and the culture of corruption. But this leads to the more general question of what determines

96

the emotional "costs" of lawbreaking. Obviously, our discussion so far suggests that these costs are low for people from societies where noncompliance is quite literally the norm. But what else allows people to break the law by day and still enjoy a good night's sleep?

Very often, good people do bad, self-serving things, but to lessen the ethical burden, they tell themselves stories about why their behavior wasn't really so wrong after all. Perhaps U.N. mission diplomats (like the rest of us) come up with rationalizations to justify their bad behavior.

An example can help illustrate what we have in mind here. Think about a ninety-five-pound weakling who suffers daily harassment at the hands of the high school bully. Let's call this weakling Ray and the bully Ted. Now suppose one morning Ray sees a twenty-dollar bill sitting on the school bus seat where he's *sure* his tormentor Ted has just been sitting. Why not just take it? It's only fair—in some cosmic sense—that he be compensated with at least $20 for his suffering, isn't it? What goes around comes around—right?

Well, sort of. It's still stealing—"two wrongs don't make a right," and all that. But at least from Ray's perspective, it's easy to rationalize taking the money, especially when it also happens to be in his own interest. In fact, even if Ted doesn't pick on you personally, but you're Ray's friend, you might walk away with the cash, figuring that you're serving some higher karmic purpose by punishing the class bully.

In the geopolitical analogy to our morality tale, the United States plays the role of the bully in the eyes of some. U.N. mission officials from countries that feel picked on (or ignored) by America, or countries bothered by America's role as the world's policeman, may have little psychological difficulty justifying their abuse of diplomatic privileges while they're living in the United States. It's their one chance to "stick it to 'The Man'" without worrying about the consequences.

We piggybacked on the efforts of the Pew Charitable Trusts, which collected information on attitudes toward the United States in over forty countries in 2002. The Pew surveyors asked a representative group of people in each country about the strength of their feelings toward the United States, ranging from 4 ("very unfavorable views") up to 1 ("very favorable views"). So high national scores (close to 4) reflect a very dim view of America, while low (closer to 1) reflect a positive one.

You might expect to see a fair number of 4s and 3s in the Pew data, owing to fallout from the Iraq War. However, the Pew survey was done before American tanks rolled into Baghdad, and in any event, we know from even more recent surveys that the United States remains wildly popular in many countries around the world today—though not as much as before the war. In table 4.3, where we rank the level of anti-American sentiment by country, you'll see that the United States is much-loved in some places, especially in Latin America and Africa, while it is reviled in other parts of the world—most intensely in the Middle East. But the broad brushstrokes obscure the fact that these views are not uniform across countries within each region.

The five countries with the most negative views are, in fact, all Middle Eastern, and are headed by countries that are all nominally U.S. allies—Egypt, Pakistan, Jordan, and Turkey. Note that Egypt and Pakistan also turn up near the top of the parking list of shame. More interestingly, diplomats from countries with very favorable views of the United States, even those from countries ranked among the most corrupt,

TABLE 4.3

The Countries with the Most and Least Favorable
Popular Attitudes toward the United States in 2002
(Source: Pew Surveys)

Rank	Country name	Average score unfavorable view of the U.S., from 1 (favorable) to 4 unfavorable)
Most unfavorable:		
1	EGYPT	3.67
2	PAKISTAN	3.51
3	JORDAN	3.27
4	TURKEY	3.04
5	LEBANON	2.93
6	ARGENTINA	2.77
7	BANGLADESH	2.54
8	SOUTH KOREA	2.48
9	INDONESIA	2.40
10	BOLIVIA	2.40
Most favorable:		
1	HONDURAS	1.59
2	VENEZUELA	1.67
3	GHANA	1.67
4	PHILIPPINES	1.68
5	NIGERIA	1.71
6	KENYA	1.74
7	UGANDA	1.76
8	UZBEKISTAN	1.77
9	IVORY COAST	1.79
10	GUATEMALA	1.84

commit surprisingly few parking violations on the streets of Manhattan. If we divide the world into five regions, and compare the level of diplomats' parking violations from countries with above-average versus below-average views of the United States for their region, everywhere (with the exception of Europe) diplomats from countries with unfavorable views commit many more violations than their counterparts from countries that like America.

Looking back at table 4.3, it's easy to see why this pattern might not hold within Europe: the European nations are notably absent from the lists of countries with very strong views (negative or positive) toward the United States, so the differences within Europe are relatively slight. As a result, other factors (such as corruption) are more important in explaining European diplomats' behavior. But elsewhere—and especially in the case of the Middle East—we find that diplomats from America-hating countries are much more inclined to park where they please in New York.[9]

We've found that diplomats from countries that dislike the United States feel that New York City parking rules "don't apply to them." Of course liking or disliking the United States shouldn't have any direct effect on corruption among government officials back in the home country. But there still may be some lessons here for understanding corruption at home.

In particular, these findings hint at the role of government officials' sentiments towards their own country's laws. Imagine two countries, one in which there is a strong sense of national pride and another where these sentiments are swamped by competing ethnic, tribal, and religious loyalties. Officials in the country with a weak sense of national identity will have an easier time justifying lawbreaking behavior to themselves since they'll have no trouble dismissing their country's laws as illegitimate (much like the diplomats in New York who have a low regard for the United States). Taking the next step in this logical chain, the strength of patriotic feelings in a society may affect how well government officials perform and thus how well government institutions function.

We do have some direct evidence on the role national pride might play in controlling corruption—albeit in a rather self-referential way. When our U.N. parking tickets research came out in an academic paper in 2006, it was picked up by journalists around the world, including one from Estonia.[10] While Estonia didn't fare too badly in our global rankings, as you can see in the table at the end of this chapter, Estonian diplomats were the worst parking violators relative to their Baltic and Scandinavian neighbors. The Estonian press was not pleased, expressing embarrassment at the behavior of their emissaries; we suspect many Estonians would share this sense of dishonor.

But what happens when, unlike the contrite Estonians, there is no strong sense of national pride (or shame)? Many observers of the economic and political disasters that have overtaken sub-Saharan Africa (which we'll turn to in the next chapter) have commented on the weakness of national identities and sentiment in many African countries. Just think about something as simple as the name of the Central African Republic. Does that sound like something people chose for themselves to express their sense of nationhood, or one imposed by a French colonial bureaucrat? Most of the forty-odd African countries south of the Sahara were stitched together during the European "Scramble for Africa" in the 1880s with no attention to language, ethnicity, or history. Given the resulting lack of patriotism in these new and artificial states, perhaps it should not surprise anyone that African corruption levels—the plundering of states by their own officials—are arguably the worst in the world. The role sentiments play in the parking decisions of U.N. diplomats offers a microcosm of this same phenomenon.

The Bottom Line on Corruption

The central lesson from New York City's parking travails with diplomats is that reformers of government institutions—whether local officials or World Bank hotshots—must be aware that values and social norms can undermine their attempts at change. In other words, altering the law is unlikely to be sufficient in the presence of a pervasive culture of corruption. Indeed, reformers are apt to face a wall of resistance from the government's own law enforcers.

The World Bank's ex-president, former U.S. Undersecretary of Defense Paul Wolfowitz, made stamping out corruption in poor countries a personal crusade, the cornerstone to what he hoped would be his legacy at the Bank. But the parking violations study offers a cautionary tale for international aid donors who, like Wolfowitz, aim to reduce corruption in developing countries: corrupt behavior is deeply engrained in culture and no small matter to root out. The standard prescriptions of economic rewards and punishments may not be enough.

We end where we began, with this chapter's opening story of one quixotic crusader's successful attempts to bring order to the once lawless, violent, and chaotic city of Bogotá, Colombia. While the behavior of U.N. diplomats implies that culture matters and is very persistent, the right response is not to give up. Culture can be changed, albeit with creativity, ingenuity, and great effort. As much may perhaps be learned from an eccentric Colombian professor-turned-mayor as from policy gurus focused on changing the economic incentives that encourage corruption.

> ### Economic Incentives Revisited: A Brief History of Parking in Manhattan
>
> It's something of an oversimplification to say that diplomats are completely above New York City's parking laws. The diplomatic right to park "any place, any time" has been a source of conflict between city governments and the United Nations since the early years of the organization. In the 1960s, former Congressman John Lindsay took over the mayor's office with a mind to cleaning up New York's traffic problems in general, and diplomats in particular. Even back then, diplomats' illegally parked vehicles clogged the streets around the United Nations and throughout the midtown box bounded by 59th Street, 34th Street, Fifth Avenue, and the East River.
>
> While recognizing that diplomatic immunity protected the illegal parkers against having to pay tickets or having their cars impounded, one of Mayor Lindsay's staffers discovered a useful loophole: an illegally parked diplomat's car could be towed to a legal parking space. The rules, moreover, did not require this spot to be nearby—it could be anywhere in Manhattan!
>
> And so, in late January 1967, diplomatic parking violators discovered that their illegally parked cars were disappearing from the curbsides in front of the

Plaza and the Russian Tea Room, and reappearing in legal spaces on the far West Side near Manhattan's rat-infested docks. The United Nations immediately filed a complaint with the U.S. State Department demanding that the city lay off their cars, and the mayor was forced to back down.

Thus began four decades of saber rattling between New York City mayors and the holders of diplomatic privilege. The parking problem had reached its peak when we began our study, with diplomats generating nearly 160,000 violations in 1996 alone. The mayor at the time, Rudy Giuliani, took an aggressive tack (as he did on most matters), making frequent threats to tow scofflaw vehicles. But he was again successfully prevented from following through by the State Department, which feared it would create international ill will. The State Department brokered agreements that were meant to settle the matter, which were all subsequently ignored by the diplomatic community.

In November 2001, Giuliani handed the problem off to Michael Bloomberg,. who has somehow succeeded where so many had failed. In September 2002, with the State Department's blessing, New York City revoked the diplomatic plates of 185 consular vehicles with more than three outstanding violations, and obtained permission to remove the plates from the vehicles of other U.N. missions' diplomats with more than three violations.[11] Evidently, it's not *just* culture that matters—blunt economic incentives matter a lot, too: U.N. diplomats' parking violations dropped by over 95 percent overnight when this new agreement went into effect.

At first blush, this seems to support the economist's view that individual incentives matter most. But as Antanas Mockus proved in Bogotá, "culture matters" and "incentives matter" are not mutually exclusive ideas, and probably reinforce each other. Keep in mind that many countries will not have the luxury of increasing legal enforcement at will, à la Mayor Bloomberg. In most places with an all-pervading norm of flouting the law, reform may be undermined by a culture of corruption among the law enforcers themselves.

CHAPTER 4 APPENDIX
Average Unpaid Annual New York City Parking Violations
per Diplomat, 11/1997 to 11/2002

Parking violations rank	Country name	Violations per diplomat, pre-enforcement	U.N. mission diplomats in 1998	Corruption index, 1998
1	KUWAIT	249.4	9	-1.07
2	EGYPT	141.4	24	0.25
3	CHAD	125.9	2	0.84
4	SUDAN	120.6	7	0.75
5	BULGARIA	119.0	6	0.50
6	MOZAMBIQUE	112.1	5	0.77
7	ALBANIA	85.5	3	0.92
8	ANGOLA	82.7	9	1.05
9	SENEGAL	80.2	11	0.45
10	PAKISTAN	70.3	13	0.76

(continued)

CHAPTER 4 APPENDIX (*cont.*)

Parking violations rank	Country name	Violations per diplomat, pre-enforcement	U.N. mission diplomats in 1998	Corruption index, 1998
11	IVORY COAST	68.0	10	0.35
12	ZAMBIA	61.2	9	0.56
13	MOROCCO	60.8	17	0.10
14	ETHIOPIA	60.4	10	0.25
15	NIGERIA	59.4	25	1.01
16	SYRIA	53.3	12	0.58
17	BENIN	50.4	8	0.76
18	ZIMBABWE	46.2	14	0.13
19	CAMEROON	44.1	8	1.11
20	MONTENEGRO & SERBIA	38.5	6	0.97
21	BAHRAIN	38.2	7	−0.41
22	BURUNDI	38.2	3	0.80
23	MALI	37.9	5	0.58
24	INDONESIA	36.5	25	0.95
25	GUINEA	35.2	5	0.57
26	BOSNIA-HERZEGOVINA	34.9	6	0.35
27	SOUTH AFRICA	34.5	19	−0.42
28	SAUDI ARABIA	34.2	12	−0.35
29	BANGLADESH	33.4	8	0.40
30	BRAZIL	30.3	33	−0.10
31	SIERRA LEONE	25.9	4	0.72
32	ALGERIA	25.6	13	0.70
33	THAILAND	24.8	13	0.26
34	KAZAKHSTAN	21.4	9	0.86
35	MAURITIUS	20.7	4	−0.20
36	NIGER	20.2	3	0.88
37	CZECH REPUBLIC	19.1	7	−0.35
38	LESOTHO	19.1	6	−0.03
39	BOTSWANA	18.7	8	−0.53

Parking violations rank	Country name	Violations per diplomat, pre-enforcement	U.N. mission diplomats in 1998	Corruption index, 1998
40	BHUTAN	18.6	5	−0.46
41	SRI LANKA	17.1	5	0.24
42	CHILE	16.7	14	−1.20
43	TUNISIA	16.7	11	−0.11
44	NEPAL	16.7	6	0.59
45	IRAN	15.9	20	0.63
46	FIJI	15.7	3	−0.20
47	ITALY	14.8	16	−1.00
48	LIBERIA	13.7	6	1.44
49	MALAWI	13.2	6	0.50
50	PARAGUAY	13.2	6	0.97
51	RWANDA	13.1	3	0.55
52	UKRAINE	13.1	14	0.89
53	SPAIN	12.9	15	−1.59
54	PHILIPPINES	11.7	20	0.26
55	GHANA	11.4	10	0.44
56	MAURITANIA	11.3	5	0.29
57	GUINEA BISSAU	10.9	10	0.82
58	ESTONIA	10.7	3	−0.49
59	MONGOLIA	10.3	5	0.28
60	ARMENIA	10.2	4	0.71
61	COSTA RICA	10.2	19	−0.71
62	COMOROS	10.1	3	0.80
63	KAMPUCHEA (CAMBODIA)	10.0	5	1.27
64	TOGO	10.0	5	0.45
65	VIETNAM	10.0	15	0.60
66	GEORGIA	9.8	8	0.64
67	CHINA (PRC)	9.6	69	0.14
68	YEMEN	9.2	8	0.57
69	VENEZUELA	9.2	16	0.77

(continued)

CHAPTER 4 APPENDIX (*cont.*)

Parking violations rank	*Country name*	*Violations per diplomat, pre- enforcement*	*U.N. mission diplomats in 1998*	*Corruption index, 1998*
70	PORTUGAL	8.9	16	−1.56
71	UZBEKISTAN	8.9	5	0.98
72	MADAGASCAR	8.8	8	0.80
73	TANZANIA	8.4	8	0.95
74	LIBYA	8.3	9	0.91
75	KENYA	7.8	17	0.92
76	CONGO (BRAZZAVILLE)	7.8	6	0.99
77	CROATIA	6.6	9	0.33
78	DJIBOUTI	6.5	3	0.80
79	SLOVAK REPUBLIC	6.5	12	0.08
80	DEMOCRATIC REPUBLIC OF CONGO (ZAIRE)	6.4	6	1.58
81	FRANCE	6.2	29	−1.75
82	INDIA	6.2	18	0.17
83	LAOS	6.2	9	0.70
84	TURKMENISTAN	5.9	4	1.13
85	PAPUA NEW GUINEA	5.6	3	0.70
86	HONDURAS	5.5	6	0.75
87	SLOVENIA	5.3	8	−0.83
88	KYRGYZSTAN	5.2	5	0.69
89	NICARAGUA	4.9	9	0.75
90	URUGUAY	4.5	11	−0.42
91	SWAZILAND	4.4	7	0.19
92	TAJIKISTAN	4.4	4	1.12
93	NAMIBIA	4.3	11	−0.24
94	MEXICO	4.0	19	0.39
95	ARGENTINA	4.0	19	0.22

Parking violations rank	Country name	Violations per diplomat, pre-enforcement	U.N. mission diplomats in 1998	Corruption index, 1998
96	SINGAPORE	3.6	6	-2.50
97	ROMANIA	3.6	10	0.38
98	UGANDA	3.5	7	0.62
99	HUNGARY	3.3	8	-0.69
100	MACEDONIA	3.3	1	0.30
101	BOLIVIA	3.1	9	0.41
102	PERU	3.1	9	0.17
103	HAITI	3.0	9	0.85
104	JORDAN	3.0	9	-0.21
105	BELARUS	2.7	8	0.60
106	BELGIUM	2.7	14	-1.23
107	CYPRUS	2.5	11	-1.38
108	GUYANA	2.3	5	0.26
109	AUSTRIA	2.2	21	-2.02
110	GABON	2.2	8	0.90
111	RUSSIA	2.1	86	0.69
112	LITHUANIA	2.1	7	-0.07
113	EL SALVADOR	1.7	10	0.27
114	POLAND	1.7	17	-0.49
115	GAMBIA	1.5	8	0.49
116	MALAYSIA	1.4	13	-0.73
117	TRINIDAD AND TOBAGO	1.4	6	-0.13
118	LEBANON	1.4	3	0.32
119	GERMANY	1.0	52	-2.21
120	ERITREA	0.8	3	-0.46
121	MOLDOVA	0.7	4	0.51
122	KOREA (SOUTH)	0.4	33	-0.11
123	DOMINICAN REPUBLIC	0.1	22	0.53
124	FINLAND	0.1	18	-2.55

(continued)

CHAPTER 4 APPENDIX (*cont.*)

Parking violations rank	Country name	Violations per diplomat, pre-enforcement	U.N. mission diplomats in 1998	Corruption index, 1998
125	GUATEMALA	0.1	9	0.63
126	SWITZERLAND	0.1	10	−2.58
127	NEW ZEALAND	0.1	8	−2.55
128	UNITED KING-DOM	0.0	31	−2.33
129	NETHERLANDS	0.0	17	−2.48
130	UNITED ARAB EMIRATES	0.0	3	−0.78
131	AUSTRALIA	0.0	12	−2.21
132	AZERBAIJAN	0.0	5	1.01
133	BURKINA-FASO	0.0	5	0.51
134	CENTRAL AFRICAN REPUB.	0.0	3	0.55
135	CANADA	0.0	24	−2.51
136	COLOMBIA	0.0	16	0.61
137	DENMARK	0.0	17	−2.57
138	ECUADOR	0.0	9	0.74
139	GREECE	0.0	21	−0.85
140	IRELAND	0.0	10	−2.15
141	ISRAEL	0.0	15	−1.41
142	JAMAICA	0.0	9	0.26
143	JAPAN	0.0	47	−1.16
144	LATVIA	0.0	5	0.10
145	NORWAY	0.0	12	−2.35
146	OMAN	0.0	5	−0.89
147	PANAMA	0.0	8	0.28
148	SWEDEN	0.0	19	−2.55
149	TURKEY	0.0	25	0.01

NOTE: The corruption index is from Kaufmann et al (2005). A higher score in the corruption index denotes more corruption.

Chapter Five

No Water, No Peace

"Oh come, come to me, beautiful rain"
—Ladysmith Black Mambazo

The Once Mighty Lake Chad

Lake Chad has disappeared. The lake, which had nurtured the land-locked people of Chad in the Sahel region of central Africa for all of recorded time—providing its surrounding inhabitants with fresh fish, water for drinking and irrigation, and a waterway for regional trade—vanished in a matter of decades. In the 1950s Lake Chad, at 25,000 square kilometers, was the sixth largest lake in the world, the size of Lake Erie or Lake Ontario. Today Lake Chad is more of a muddy pond than a real lake, expanding and receding with the rains, teasing locals who remember and long for its former grandeur. Most of the fish died long ago and middle-aged fishermen whose ancestors had plied the lake for generations have had to abandon their way of life altogether. Former fishing ports now lie stranded in the desert, with boats listing on their sides over fifty miles away from the mud that currently passes as lakefront.

As irrigation becomes more difficult and the local climate dries out, agricultural production has also suffered. Chad's cattle pastoralists have been forced to move south or east into wetter climes by the expanding desert, sometimes provoking conflicts with the tribes that already farm those lands. As Muhammadu Bello, a former fisherman forced into subsistence farming, laments, "This lake is dying and we are dying with it."[1]

The disappearance of Lake Chad is emblematic of Africa's twin crises of poverty and conflict. In contrast to its proud past of empires, artisans, and trade, Chad is now filled with the ghostly figures of fishermen without a lake, farmers plowing barren fields, pastoralists wandering the desert for days in search of shrub for their cattle to eat. It's one of the poorest countries on earth, and apparently one of the most corrupt, based on the parking behavior of their U.N. diplomats in New York City. As its economic decline has accelerated, so has its political turmoil. Chad has experienced almost continuous civil war since its independence from France in 1960. Conflict has raged in every year but two since 1964, and things are only getting worse. A recent major flare-up of violence has seen competing rebel bandits struggling for power with the government and one another.

It's a war that's often fought by child soldiers abducted by rebels and government leaders alike. Much of the time, though, new recruits willingly sign on for the fight. When all of the fish are dead and drought has killed off the crops, a young Chadian has little to lose by joining a rebel band, no matter how brutal. He may actually eke out a better living from stolen loot than by going it alone, especially since farmers who aren't linked to any armed group are easy prey for the rebels or the national army. In the name of survival, we'd probably do the same thing if we walked in their shoes. The calculus of survival can turn anyone into an economic gangster.

The presence of longstanding ethnic divisions further muddies the picture. Religious, language, and racial divides form the fault lines of today's conflict. Chad's south is mainly Christian and black, while northerners look to the Arab and Muslim worlds for identity and inspiration. Until the start of French colonial rule in the late nineteenth century, much of Chad's black African population was enslaved by Muslim northerners, and not just by a privileged elite: even working class Muslim fishermen on Lake Chad owned black slaves.

Chad seems caught in a "conflict trap": poverty drives a desperate population to armed violence; armed violence begets more poverty; and the growing economic desperation generates ever more recruits for warring factions. Soon people come to believe that the conflict will never end. And if that's the case, why tend cattle that will just end up being stolen? Why cultivate crops that will be razed by marauders? As farmers abandon farming and herders kill their flocks, Chadians are stuck in the ever-tightening grip of poverty and violence.

Unfortunately, much of sub-Saharan Africa looks like Chad, and in the recurring cycles of poverty and conflict traps, it's impossible to sort out what's causing what. Is widespread civil war in Africa an unwelcome symptom of its grinding poverty—or is it the other way around? Or both? We have to know the answer if we hope to do anything about it. But without some idea of its leading causes, we'll never be able help Chad and others figure out how to break this cycle.

We cannot come up with a complete accounting for violence in Chad or elsewhere. But we can use our economic tools to zero in on one unlikely culprit. Not the CIA, not Christian-Muslim tensions, not overpopulation. A bigger problem is the weather. Rainfall, it turns out, is key for both our economic analysis and also Africa's recent history of violence: more wars break out when the rains fail. And while we can't control the weather, knowing that it's at the root of civil conflict may help us to figure out how to finally end Africa's perfect storm of violence and poverty.

The Scourge of Armed Conflict

Chad is not alone in its troubles. The scale of armed violence worldwide is simply staggering. Rich countries don't have civil wars anymore but dozens of poor countries have had conflicts as brutal as Chad's. In many places war is more common than peace. The majority of the world's countries have had civil war on their soil since 1980 and most are concentrated in the developing regions of Africa, Asia, and Latin America.[2]

Africa is the unfortunate standout, home to both the highest number of wars and the bloodiest. Millions of civilians have died over the past two decades. The seemingly endless list of wars—in Angola, Liberia, Mozambique, Rwanda, Sierra Leone, Somalia, Sudan, Burundi, Chad, both Congos (Democratic Republic of Congo and Republic of Congo), Ethiopia, Eritrea, Cote d'Ivoire, Niger, Uganda—evokes nightmarish images of massacres, blood diamonds, gang rapes, and heavily armed and drugged-up child soldiers tormenting motorists at checkpoints.

It's a gruesome but essential exercise to go through the

numbers to grasp the urgency of putting an end to Africa's wars. Over 50,000 people died in Sierra Leone's civil war between 1991 and 2002, and millions were displaced from their homes by the ruthless Revolutionary United Front (RUF) rebels. The RUF's calling card was the amputation of the hands of civilians for nothing other than being in the wrong place at the wrong time. The Democratic Republic of Congo's ongoing war has been even bloodier, with three million civilians thought to be dead.[3] The Darfur genocide is just the latest chapter in Sudan's never-ending war that has cost the lives of countless millions. Nearly a million died in the 1994 Rwandan genocide, over 10 percent of the country's entire population. Each of these civilian death tolls is an order of magnitude higher than the worst that American civilians have ever experienced in war.

As the battles of one country spill over into other nations, both near and far, wars breed more war. Conflicts jump borders as armed fighters seek out new sources of loot and small arms which, seemingly through osmosis, permeate a region. As a result of the carnage in Darfur, refugees have flooded over the border into eastern Chad, disrupting the normal trading patterns that brought at least some economic activity to the region. Sierra Leone's civil war was started by a cross-border raid by Liberian rebels covetous of diamond fields near their common border, sparking a war that engulfed Sierra Leone for a decade. Following the 1994 genocide, hundreds of thousands of desperate Rwandan refugees flowed into the Democratic Republic of Congo, providing an opening for a long dormant rebel movement that finally toppled Congo's notorious dictator Mobutu in 1997. But then other rebels arose to fight these new rulers, starting a conflict that continues to fester at the time of this book's writing.

Neighboring countries—Angola, Rwanda, Uganda, and Zimbabwe—sent their troops to Congo with designs on its vast mineral wealth.

Neither are we in the world's rich countries immune to the global aftershocks of civil war, which can emerge in terrifying ways. Failed states can provide a lawless sanctuary for international organized crime and terrorist groups that profit from the illicit trades in arms, drugs, and rare minerals, like diamonds. Conflict zones in Afghanistan and Colombia serve as bases for major international drug *narcotraficantes*. Al-Qaeda operatives set up shop in Sudan and Sierra Leone during the 1990s and more recently in Somalia. States destroyed by terror and violence beget further suffering. Chad's wars are not just Chad's business.

While it gets lost in the wash of individual stories and in the numbing casualty statistics, a lot of what we've described sounds like people making economic trade-offs. When the future becomes hopeless and you have nothing to lose, why not take up arms? When resources are scarce, do the gains from fighting for control over these resources outweigh the risks of slow starvation? If economic trade-offs lie behind these problems, perhaps economics can help us find some answers.

Hatred or Poverty?

Because making sense of the atrocities of war can seem downright impossible, many observers focus on irrational and ancient tribal hatreds as the root causes of civil wars in Africa and elsewhere. Journalists who parachute in to cover the conflicts take it as self-evident that ethnic rivalry is the source of any violence they observe. And some civil wars—at first glance, at least—do seem to correspond to this view.

That's certainly what we heard in the final analysis of the 1994 Rwandan genocide, where Hutu radicals slaughtered nearly a million (although no one really knows the exact number—see the textbox below, "Data: The First Casualty of War") of their Tutsi neighbors and Hutu political opponents over the course of only three months. This was a premeditated massacre on a scale not seen since the Nazi Holocaust of the 1940s.

But this view, repeated so often as to be held as fact rather than conjecture, has obscured the critical role that economic factors can play in sparking violence between ethnic groups. In fact, recent research shows that outright ethnic warfare—like Rwanda—is much more the exception than the rule.[4] Many civil wars actually take place in ethnically homogeneous societies. Somalia—one of the world's *least* diverse countries in terms of language, religion, race, and culture—is a more typical case. Fighting there takes place among rival clans (essentially extended families) who look, dress, talk, and pray pretty much the same way. But Somalia's uniformity obviously hasn't brought its people peace. Even in some countries with many distinct groups, such as Sierra Leone, fault lines in their civil wars largely bypassed ethnic and religious boundaries. The notorious RUF rebels came from all of Sierra Leone's different ethnic groups and didn't discriminate in choosing who they massacred throughout the country. The war was terrifying—but not tribal.

Even Rwanda deserves a second look. The main trigger of violence may have been as much economic as ethnic, resting in its commercial links to the outside world. As a nation, Rwanda is heavily dependent on coffee exports, and many if not most families earn a livelihood harvesting coffee beans on fertile but crowded hillsides. World coffee prices plunged from 1989 to 1993 by more than 50 percent, as Vietnam put ever more land into coffee production and a recession in espresso-addicted countries dampened demand.[5] Rwandan peasants were just barely scraping by before the coffee collapse. With the price of their main crop cut in half, many now stared hunger squarely in the eye, causing extreme economic circumstances that probably helped the Hutu government rally a desperate public behind its calls for genocide.

Are economic or cultural factors mainly to blame for this recent history of violence? Rwanda suggests both are important. But rather than continuing to recite individual anecdotes and cases that yield no consistent pattern, we'll turn to the data.

Data: The First Casualty of War

You'd think that at least measuring violence wouldn't be too hard. We can figure out where wars are occurring just by tuning into the nightly news, and wars unfortunately produce large and very visible body counts. But the casualty figures you read in the newspaper are almost always guesses, and not very educated ones at that. During the chaos of war, few societies have functioning newspapers or statistical agencies to tally up the damage and count the body bags (let alone to keep track of normal aggregate economic statistics like national income, inflation, or exports). Humanitarian agencies are stretched too thin with the immediate task of saving lives to worry about data collection. Often the only casualty estimates are released by the fighting groups themselves, so we end up back at the "cheap talk" problem with measuring violence just as we did with corruption.

The recent controversy over civilian deaths in Iraq highlights some of these difficulties. Compared to the remote jungles of Congo, counting casualties in Iraq should be child's play. Iraq is a middle-income country, much richer than most of Africa, and has a large bureaucracy. And what do bureaucracies do if not churn out reams of statistics? There are hundreds of thousands of U.S. troops, contractors, and administrators on the ground and nonstop international media coverage. Yet there's still little agreement on the number of civilian casualties suffered so far.

U.S. government casualty reports have regularly come in far below independent estimates, sometimes by a very wide margin. While U.S. government reports estimated 2003–04 civilian casualties at around ten thousand, a study by Johns Hopkins University researchers placed the civilian toll at over 100,000.[6] Debate over the correct statistical approach in measuring the carnage in Iraq was immediately overshadowed by the politics of these numbers, much as civilian casualty estimates during the Vietnam War were controversial for an earlier generation. Similarly, despite a media spotlight of its own, the Darfur genocide is still a black box of unmeasured slaughter.

Civil conflicts have other data casualties. The breakdown of government institutions during war means that many African countries lack even basic national population and economic information. In some, a census hasn't been carried out in decades.[7] The first proper national population census in Chad was only conducted in 1993, more than three decades after independence from France. No census has taken place since then and, given its smoldering war and refugee crisis, none will be taken for the foreseeable future. War-torn Angola has not carried out a population census since its independence from Portugal in 1974 (although with the arrival of peace in 2002, this may change). The planned 1993 national population census in Sudan was cancelled because of the civil war in the south. All told, this means we know a lot less than we need to know about societies at war.

Without casualty figures, we can't measure the scale of conflict. So we'll just look for the onset of war—either there is fighting or there isn't in our data. As we'll see below, that's all we'll need, along with a little help from some meteorologists.

Rainfall

Rich countries don't have many wars, especially not civil ones. That's our first hint that economic factors really matter. If we look at countries with 1979 per capita income above $10,000 (like the United States, Japan, and Germany) and those with incomes below $1,000 (most of Africa and much of Asia), a stark pattern emerges: in any given year, armed civil conflict is *six times* more likely in the world's poor countries.[8] Civil conflicts are almost unknown in the countries of the Organisation for Economic Cooperation and Development (OECD), the political country club of the world's wealthy nations. Among the poor countries of the world, it's a shockingly different story: two thirds of African countries and nearly as high a fraction in Asia have had armed conflicts since 1980.

War doesn't simply fall from the sky. It's created by people, perhaps as a result of their desperate economic conditions. And poverty doesn't appear out of nowhere, either. It arises at least in part because of violent conditions where no one wants to invest or produce anything. It's clear that war and poverty go hand in hand. But to understand whether economic deprivation really is at the root of Africa's wars, we would ideally require that some countries become richer owing to nothing other than random chance, and that some other countries become poorer simply due to bad luck. Then we could see if these unexpected changes in economic circumstances that "fall from the sky" create violence in the poor countries and peace in the richer ones.

Since countries aren't lab rats and we can't play with levels of global poverty from our office computers, we need to wait for nature to create changes that we can study as if they were a real laboratory experiment. In this case, it turns out that our falling-from-the-sky metaphor isn't really a metaphor at all. Sometimes poverty *does* fall from the sky, literally, in the form of rain. The majority of Africans today still rely on rain-fed agriculture to make a living. Irrigation systems and water storage are rare, so when the rains don't arrive, crops wither and die, leaving farmers without anything to eat or the means to purchase other basic necessities. Sometimes, though, you can have too much of a good thing: if the rains are too heavy, flooding can also wash away livelihoods.

When rainfall doesn't cooperate, African farmers' corn, sorghum, and cotton production collapses, leaving them desperate or even destitute. Herders can be hit just as hard as farmers. During the 2005 Sahel drought, sixty-four-year-old Malian herder Houtafa Ag Moussa lost most of his herd to the drought. He describes his situation rather starkly, "The rain has stopped and the grass isn't growing. . . . If there is no rain, the rest of my animals will die . . . and so will we."[9] Households then face some very uncomfortable choices: stay put or migrate in search of food? Pay school fees for children or deny them an education? Give the one remaining cup of cornmeal porridge to an adult or to a child? People will do whatever it takes to survive. It's certainly not irrational for those with nothing left to lose to join the ranks of criminals or rebels to get their share of what little there is to eat in a hungry nation (especially when lured to fight by charismatic economic gangsters with promises of wealth, status, and power, not to mention food).

If we believe that a direct link connects poverty and violence, then when failing rains create economic hardship, war should follow. In this case, we can actually figure out whether poverty *caused* violence by isolating rainfall's effects: whether rain falls from the sky is independent of the battles waged by humans on the ground and any other sources of feast or famine in the local economy.

Feast, Famine, and Africa's Legacy of Violence

Together with our colleagues Shanker Satyanath and Ernesto Sergenti at New York University, we went about answering this all-important question of whether droughts—extreme declines in rainfall from one year to the next—cause armed civil conflict.[10] Unfortunately, there isn't much information on rainfall. Many African countries don't maintain enough ground rainfall gauges to accurately measure precipitation, and without rainfall data we can't even tell where and when there have been droughts, let alone figure out whether it triggered local fighting. But since the late 1970s, satellites have also been able to measure local rainfall.[11] The satellite data rely on a combination of ground weather stations and satellite information on what is called "cold cloud cover" density, which is closely related to actual precipitation.[12] These estimated rainfall data show just how desperate the situation is for our African farmers. It's common for African countries to average two or even three drought years each decade, and overall rainfall variability in African countries like Chad, Kenya, and Sudan is several times higher than in the United States.[13]

What's in a Name?

In Kenya, where Ted has done fieldwork, many people name their kids after events taking place at the time of birth. Sometimes this means a major international or national event—kids born in 1964, Kenya's independence year, were often named "Uhuru," which means "freedom" in Swahili—but local events are most common. Common events result in common names. It's a sad but telling indication of the harsh lives of many Kenyans that one of the most typical boy's names in the Luhya language dominant in western Kenya is "Wanjala," meaning "born in a time of hunger," derived from the word for hunger (*njaa*).

When rains fail, so do the crops, and in an agrarian society, as the harvest goes, so goes the economy. That's clear enough. More remarkably, though, we also find a very strong relationship between drought and civil conflict in Africa. An armed civil conflict is much more likely the year after a large rainfall drop than in normal years. Since droughts cannot possibly be caused by civil war, we can be confident that civil wars are more likely to occur after major economic shocks like droughts rather than vice versa.

Drought and the resulting economic hardship turn out to matter a lot for understanding African conflict. A 1 percent decline in national GDP increases the likelihood of civil conflict by about 2 percentage points. So an income drop of 5 percent—a large but altogether common deterioration in economic conditions, especially when the rains fail—increases the risk of civil conflict in the following year to roughly 30 percent, up from an already high average probability of conflict of around 20 percent in normal rainfall years. Just imagine living in a place where next year there is nearly a one in three chance that you'll be living in a war zone. Never mind that your crops have failed, so you already have your hands full just finding your next meal.

Another striking finding emerges from the analysis. Political and social factors don't seem to dampen the core role of economic shocks in generating violence. African countries are equally at risk of violence after droughts whether they are democracies or dictatorships, ethnically homogeneous or split by tribal and religious divisions, or socialist or capitalist in their economic policies. Poverty increases the risk of armed conflict for all Africans.

While economic desperation is not the *only* cause of

armed violence in Africa, it's remarkably important. Based on our calculations, African countries may have as much as 50 percent more risk of war (the jump from roughly 20 percent to 30 percent above) in years of economic recession than in other years. Other factors surely matter—ethnic divisions in some places and political oppression in others. And while we can't make more rain fall, smoothing out the ups and downs of African incomes would be a major step forward in our fight against the continent's wars.

In theory, the farmers themselves could take steps to iron out the highs and lows of the annual harvest cycle. After all, that's the purpose of an insurance policy; you would pay a premium at the beginning of the planting season to guarantee some minimal level of income even if the rains never come. Or if crops fail, you could just take out a bank loan that you'd pay back in a better harvest year. But formal insurance policies and banking institutions are almost unknown in African villages. There are very few banks in the African countryside, in large part because farmers don't have collateral assets they can put up to secure loans.

A little neighborly assistance could also serve as insurance against a bad year. If you help me when I need a hand, I'll return the favor when you fall on hard times. But while neighbors do help their neighbors in Africa (as they do everywhere), local mutual assistance is of little use when a major drought strikes an entire region, leaving all households scrambling to tend to their own needs and in no position to provide neighborly help.

Many African households do save some grain from the previous harvest, in part to seed their next crop. They can also "save" by purchasing cattle or other assets they can sell—or at least eat—in difficult times, much the same way that we might draw down a savings account or sell off a certificate of deposit. But minor measures like these are insufficient to feed a whole family for a year when an entire harvest is lost. Yale economist Chris Udry found that households' accumulated savings could only make up for about one quarter of the income drop they experienced during the severe droughts in West Africa's Burkina Faso in the 1980s.[14] The remaining three quarters of the short-fall translated directly into lower spending on essential items like food and medicine.

This lack of insurance for poor African farmers is particularly tragic since they have much greater need for help than farmers elsewhere. Sub-Saharan Africa faces far more frequent droughts than other tropical regions as a result of global climate patterns, the continent's shape, the position of mountain ranges, and other accidents of geography.[15] It's one of the ironies of modern finance that the tools that could most help the poor are least readily available to them.

A stark illustration of drought-as-trigger is the recent war in Niger, Chad's western neighbor in the bone-dry Sahel. Niger is home to the pastoralist Tuareg ethnic group. The car company Volkswagen appropriated their name for a highly successful crossover SUV, but the tribe itself hasn't been so lucky. Their herds were devastated by a series of ever deeper droughts in the 1970s and 1980s.[16] Initially, the Tuareg responded to the loss of livelihood by migrating north in large numbers to Algeria and Libya in search of better living conditions, defusing the imminent threat of conflict.

They didn't find a warm welcome in their new homes either and by the late 1980s many thousands were repatriated to Niger, just in time for another round of severe droughts in 1989 and 1990. The Tuareg, starving and resentful in the face of what they considered to be insufficient resettlement assistance from the state, began fighting with the government, a conflict that only grew worse as the rains continued to fail: five of the seven years after 1990 were dry, and the conflict between the Tuaregs and the state intensified and spread. The conflict ended—temporarily—in 1998, and the country enjoyed a short window of peace until 2001. Perhaps the rain gods can be thanked for this reprieve from the fighting: in three of the four years between 1998 and 2001, rising rainfall levels were sufficient to produce ample harvests.

Unfortunately, the rains have recently failed again and peace has unraveled. The country suffered a massive drought in 2004, followed by locust pestilence and famine in 2005. Crop prices skyrocketed and untold thousands died. At this point, you can make a pretty decent guess as to what came next: Niger's government is today back at war with the Tuareg militia, the Niger Movement for Justice, which has recently scored some major military strikes, including the capture and killing of government troops and even the destruction of a regional airport in 2007.[17] The unfortunate citizens of Niger, as ever caught in the crossfire, can only pray for rain.

The Threat of Global Warming

Unlike Niger, China's economy is booming. In 1978, 70 percent of China's billion people were farmers, working the land in cooperatives created during the Communist government's Great Leap Forward (which in retrospect was anything but). Market-oriented reforms have since produced an astounding industrial transformation. The countryside has started to empty as China's rural masses seek their fortunes in coastal cities. More than twice as many Chinese lived in

127

urban areas in 2005 than they did twenty-five years earlier, when the reforms began. This economic miracle has brought higher living standards to hundreds of millions of people in a few short decades: China's income per capita was at African levels in the 1970s before the reforms, but now workers there earn many times as much as their African counterparts.

But China's modern economic growth is fuelled, literally, by burning coal, gas, and oil. The torrid rate of expansion of Chinese manufacturing is outstripped only by its growing fossil fuel consumption. Between 2002 and 2004, energy use in China increased by a staggering 33 percent, and the resulting increase in carbon dioxide (CO_2) emissions made China the world's biggest polluter of greenhouse gases by 2007—far ahead of predictions for when China would edge out the United States.[18] Together, these two countries account for over 40 percent of global CO_2 emissions, the main culprit behind global warming.

The cars and trucks clogging Shanghai's new freeways seem to double every few years, and the air pollution has gotten so bad that Beijingers sometimes go months without seeing their city's once-famous blue skies. China's smoke-belching factories that feed global demand for steel, cement, shoes, and toys show no sign of slowing down—nor do American tastes for SUVs and large air-conditioned homes. So the world's CO_2 pollution numbers aren't likely to drop anytime soon.

Half a world away in Chad, Niger, and Sudan, China's manufacturing boom and America's gated suburbs may as well be on another planet but for one thing: the lives of African peasant farmers, U.S. mall-goers, and Chinese factory workers—and everyone else around the world—are connected by our collective effect on the Earth's climate. As we all continue to guzzle fossil fuels, the planet is heating up. For poor African farmers, where the weather determines whether the next harvest will yield enough food to eat, or barren fields will bring hunger, what comes out of factory smokestacks in China could truly be a matter of life and death. If changing global weather brings less rain to Africa, it may also bring more war.

Global Weathermen

Despite the lingering naysayers, scientists worldwide largely agree that climate change is happening and isn't going away anytime soon. This consensus is expressed in the United Nations scientific report called the Intergovernmental Panel on Climate Change (IPCC) Fourth Assessment, whose authors were awarded the 2007 Nobel Peace Prize (together with Al Gore). The leading researchers who penned the report agree that in the coming decades, rising global temperatures and sea levels will change life as we know it, altering landscapes and habitats across the globe.[19]

But while many experts generally agree that the planet is heating up, there are divergent views on exactly how it'll change and by how much. The U.N. report predicts that temperatures worldwide could increase by anywhere from 2.0°F to 11.5°F (1.1°C to 6.4°C) during the twenty-first century.[20] A rise in temperature of 6°F to 7°F can have a major impact on agriculture, amounting to the difference between a bountiful harvest and a failed crop. Some places will get much warmer, while others may actually see the thermometer dip despite higher average temperatures worldwide.

Who stands to gain from a hotter planet? Perhaps not

surprisingly, the list includes countries that currently suffer through long, cold, depressing winters. Higher temperatures in Siberia, Canada, and the northern United States may be a boon for agriculture, opening up vast new plains for wheat production and possibly human settlement. Even if Canadians (like Ray) lose their outdoor hockey rinks, it'd be more than compensated for by an early thaw and extra days at the beach.

But there will be global warming losers, too. Higher temperatures may spell disaster for small Pacific islands and for coastal dwellers in low-lying countries like Bangladesh—or in the city of New Orleans. But not all losers are created equal. Global climate change will have starkly different implications for the world's rich and poor countries. Wealthy nations like the United States or Canada have the financial resources to adapt to major environmental change. If temperatures rise in California, America's biggest farm state, teams of agriculture experts, like our colleagues at the University of California, will help our farmers figure out which crops are best suited to the changing conditions. Perhaps they'll even develop new plant varieties bred specifically to cope with global warming. Federal and state governments would also help out farmers whose land is no longer viable for farming, and provide insurance to those whose transitions to the new crops don't work out as planned. No one should starve in California if temperatures rise by a few degrees.

For those of us living in advanced, post-industrial—and air conditioned—societies like the United States, what do higher temperatures really mean anyway? A slightly bigger electric bill at the end of each summer month (counterbalanced with smaller heating bills in winter)? Some parts of the United States may be buffeted by stronger hurricanes and tornadoes, but climate change in the range predicted by the reputable climate models won't be catastrophic for most rich countries. Silicon Valley's idea factories and the investment banks in London, New York, and Tokyo will keep on humming if it's a few degrees warmer outside.

Climate Change and Conflict in Sahelian Africa

But Chad and its neighbors won't fare so well. They till their land each year teetering on the brink of survival. The government can't afford a safety net for farmers whose crops fail. No agricultural experts will help them shift to new crops, and given the low literacy rates, it'd be a challenge to train farmers in new farming techniques anyway. If global warming brings more droughts to Chad or its neighbors, farmers won't be able to adjust and the region's dire economic situation will only grow worse. And so will the cycle of poverty and violence that afflicts the region.

Though it's far from universal, several leading international climate scientists predict that conditions will get worse in the Sahel region of west and central Africa, a parched stretch of earth containing Chad and Niger, as well as parts of Sudan, Mali, Senegal, and their neighbors.[21] Princeton University researchers have developed a leading U.S. climate model that offers grim forecasts, predicting that in the Sahel average temperatures in the region will rise 6.3°F (3.5°C) and rainfall will drop sharply by 24 percent over the next eighty years. What little rain that does fall will evaporate more quickly due to higher temperatures. One of the driest places on earth may get a whole lot drier.

The Sahel region includes over one-hundred million of

the poorest people in the world. Average annual per capita income in the fifteen Sahelian countries is only $346. The entire region is today already racked by political instability and warfare, and if its fragile soils turn into desert sand, things can only get worse. The only question is by how much. It's the cruelest of ironies that the poorest people in the world—in the region least able to deal with extreme weather—also look like potentially the biggest losers in the global climate change lottery.

With the benefit of hindsight, it now seems obvious that the process has already begun and that the changes have been accelerating. In the last hundred years, cities like Timbuktu, Mali, have gone from flourishing trade hubs to desolate clusters of mud-brick homes engulfed by desert. The oases of Somalia on the opposite end of the continent have also dried up, leading to more frequent armed clashes between clans over scarce water resources. And then there's Lake Chad which, as we know, is almost completely gone, and if current trends continue may be just a memory in a few short decades.

Climate scientists' models predict less rain on average, but years with well below average rains will become more common as will periods of intense rainfall. Just as there are ways of coping with declining rainfall, there are also ways of dealing with the capricious year-to-year variability in rainfall. California farmers dig extensive irrigation systems to cope with drought years; levees in New Orleans were constructed to contain floods. But these are luxuries far out of reach of the African farmer, and while some crops, like cassava, do well in dry conditions, they suffer with heavy rains. Corn doesn't mind a lot of rain but withers and dies in drought years. Which crop should they plant? With the increasing capriciousness of the rain gods, more farmers will find themselves caught growing the wrong crop in the wrong year.

How much more violence do we expect to be visited on the people of the Sahel in the coming century? Remember that in Africa, conflict risk increases from roughly 20 percent to 30 percent in years when a country is hit by drought-induced economic hardship. If we knew the number of extra drought years that will hit the Sahel as a result of global warming, we'd be able to come up with an estimate of the increase in conflict risk that would follow. These estimates necessarily involve some guesswork: our economic crystal ball isn't going to give an exact conflict forecast for Africa, since the uncertainty in future climate translates into uncertainty over future conflict.

The only good news is that it's not all bad news. Since climate models are all over the place for Africa as a whole, our predictions about future conflict risk are similarly imprecise. If we average over these wildly disparate predictions, the overall effect of global warming on conflict risk in Africa is pretty much flat, though with some risk of rising conflict. In some models conflict risk actually drops slightly as rainfall conditions improve, in places like Kenya and Tanzania, for instance.

Predictions for the Sahel are equally uncertain, but according to some models the future could be very bleak. And given the disastrous consequences for the Sahel's one-hundred million people, it's worth planning for the worst. Based on the increase in droughts predicted by the Princeton climate model, the already sky-high levels of civil conflict in the Sahel—already the world's most conflict-prone region—could increase over 15 percent by 2080.

If Chinese factories and U.S. cars keep flooding the sky

with CO_2, today's brutal violence could even be remembered as "the good old days" for Sahelian countries: if carbon emissions increase in a more dramatic but still feasible pattern, the Princeton model predicts that rainfall will dwindle and conflict risk could soar by the end of the century. The weather changes caused by higher pollution trends could make life simply unlivable in many parts of the Sahel, sending millions of hungry refugees into neighboring countries in search of food and water, and making the downward spiral of poverty and violence accelerate ever faster.

Of course, these bleak predictions assume that the world will just keep on chugging along as it has been for the past thirty years or so, with China, America, and the rest of the industrialized world continuing to spew endless tons of carbon dioxide into the atmosphere; with Africans failing to make the transformation to industrialized economies; and with irrigation systems in the Sahel remaining rudimentary at best. But given the failure to change Africa's economic landscape over the past few decades, this gloomy scenario serves as a harsh warning of what the future could potentially hold, and hopefully a big kick-in-the-pants to do something about it.

Saving Darfur?

The disappearance of Lake Chad has been a pox on Chad's people, pushing them to the brink of starvation. But what if the same thing happened in reverse? Suppose we stumbled across a long-lost lake to replace Lake Chad?

That might be happening right now in Darfur, Sudan. In a story eerily similar to Chad's, only worse, perhaps 200,000 people have been killed and millions made refugees in the ongoing Darfur conflict. Most victims have been innocent civilians, terrorized by either Sudanese government-supported *janjaweed* militias or various separatist Darfuri rebel splinter factions. Recurrent droughts are again part of the complex story of conflict and bloodshed, as the spread of the Sahara Desert south into Darfur intensifies the struggle for land and water, and forces groups to relocate to survive.[22]

But if Boston University geologist Farouk el-Baz is right, the water shortage may soon be over. Using radar imaging technology, el-Baz and his colleagues claim to have found an immense underground aquifer, the remnant of an ancient lake. The underground lake may have a surface area twice the size of Lake Erie. Their plan is to dig a thousand deep borehole wells to bring the water to the surface to irrigate crops, nourish cattle, and of course give the people of Darfur something to drink.

The existence of the new lake is still a matter of intense speculation, and many experts remain unconvinced by the geological science underlying el-Baz's claims.[23] While only time will tell whether water for Darfur's desperate millions will help end the conflict there, we shouldn't underestimate the power of water in dousing violence in Africa.

Chapter Six

Death by a Thousand Small Cuts

A Gruesome Calculus

Murders, kidnappings, and car-jackings are part of daily life in the sprawling megacities of the developing world, causing the rich and privileged to retreat to lives behind high, barbed wire-topped walls. Kenya's capital got the nickname "Nairobbery" for a reason. While civil war is violence played out on a grand and tragic scale, countries spared large-scale conflict can still suffer death by a thousand small cuts in the form of violent crime.

Some of these personal tragedies have obvious economic underpinnings—the hungry and destitute naturally covet their neighbors' possessions. The fight for survival among slum dwellers drives urban crime. But a great many crimes seem to defy rational explanation altogether. What is the economic rationale for murder or rape—or child abuse? Or religious terrorism? Or the targeting of elderly women in lethal witch-hunts, which, as we'll find out, continue today in many countries, centuries after the storied Salem witch trials.

In chapter 4, we found that not everything can be explained by rational economic incentives, and that some decisions really are a matter of culture. The term "culture of violence" surely comes from somewhere, and in the domain of witch-hunters and religious warriors it would seem an apt description. But in this chapter, we'll find that some of what seems to be rooted in culture and tradition can in fact be traced back to the economic calculus of survival. Once we recognize that seemingly random acts of violence have economic underpinnings, we can use our economic toolbox to try to address the problem.

Think back to the typical rural African household whose crops have failed; food is scarce and so are the family's options. After all of last year's harvest has been eaten, the cattle sold off, and all favors from friends called in, households sometimes face some very uncomfortable arithmetic. What if there are still too many mouths and too little food?

Each household member could go his own way in search of food or work, and migration is a common response to famines. This happened seventy years ago in the United States when the Great Plains turned into a giant dustbowl, causing mass migrations to California during the Great Depression. But countries like Kenya and Chad don't have a Golden State of opportunity where fortunes can be sought by the starving masses—remember the migrations of Niger's Tuaregs from chapter 5?

Without a possibility of escaping to greener pastures, everyone in the household could instead be called upon to first cut back on what they spend and consume. While this sounds fair, it could actually make the family's situation even worse. Humans require a minimum amount of calories and nutrition just to keep their hearts beating and brains functioning, what doctors call "basal metabolism." Fall below this level of nutrition and you risk death. If distributing food equally puts everyone at risk of dipping below this critical calorie level, then an equal sharing rule could be tantamount to a death sentence for everyone in the household.

It's unsettling to consider, but under these conditions it could make a perverse kind of sense for the household to focus its resources on a few select individuals to make sure that at least they survive, albeit at the cost of endangering other household members.[1] But within these starving households, how do you make the impossible choice of who will live and who will die?

This gut-wrenching choice is something we in the rich world are thankfully spared, but it's been common throughout human history. Anthropologists studying preindustrial societies have discovered that many cultures had precise rules for allocating food during famines, and that these rules usually protected the young at the expense of the old. Many societies engaged in "death-hastening" activities for the elderly—including withdrawal of food, abandonment, or even murder—when there wasn't enough food to go around.

Among the Amassalik Inuit on the Arctic tundra, the elderly were given dramatic send-offs during lean times, with the old and decrepit abandoned on ice floes while the tribe was out fishing.[2] The Inuit are not alone: Icelanders, Amazonian Bororos, Siberian Chukchees, Fijians, North American Hopis, Gabon Fang, African San, and Australian Tiwi, among others, all accelerated the deaths of the elderly during famines. The ancient Japanese sent their elderly alone up into the mountains to die of cold or become prey for wild animals when there wasn't enough food for them. It sounds barbaric to our modern sensibilities, but then few of us have lived on the edge of subsistence where such severe traditions are almost a necessity.

Why pick on the elderly? They are often frail and incapable of defending themselves, and their income-generating capacity—whether on or off the farm—is lower than for young adults. They often produce less food (or income) than they consume, making them a net economic burden for the household. They are both the weakest contributors to group survival and also the least capable of acting in self-defense.

Elderly women are particularly at risk when they lack the political influence of males, which is true in most traditional societies. In much of rural Africa, male elders have powerful groups or local councils while women's voices are less often heard in public. Many women also move away from their birth communities and into their husbands' homes when they marry, leaving them further isolated in their old age, far from siblings and other close kin. In answer to the gruesome question of who lives and who dies, elderly women draw the short straw.

Tanzania's Witch-hunts

Meatu district is at the epicenter of a rash of "witch killing" in Tanzania. Yes, attacks on women accused of witchcraft are a regular occurrence throughout western Tanzania. In Meatu, fully *half* of all reported murders are witch killings, and hundreds of these murders take place every year in Tanzania as a whole.

In many parts of Africa and the rest of the world (including Europe and North America into the seventeenth century), witches take the blame for others' misfortunes. Poor health—blame the witch. Crop failure—blame the witch. Business problems, loss of livestock—you get the idea. And if some disaster is the witch's fault, then eliminating the witch seems a sensible way of ending the "curse" that surely lies behind any misfortune. People down on their luck in rural Tanzania frantically search for clues about who in their midst might have been casting wicked spells or otherwise placing curses on them, even for problems as mundane as a failed job search, the loss of their favorite sports team in a big game, or bad scores on school exams.

African witchcraft is an intimate crime—most accusations occur within circles of trust like family and friends. Dutch anthropologist Peter Geschiere calls African witchcraft "the dark side of kinship," since so many accusations and attacks take place within families.[3] Grandmothers and old aunts are the most common targets for these brutal attacks on suspected witches. Victims are killed with machete blows to the head, neck, and shoulders. Those women who manage to escape the attacks often flee to the bush where they die of exposure. The lucky ones make it to nearby cities where they become homeless, living off charity. Once tarnished as witches, no one in their own village will have anything to do with them. Moving elsewhere usually isn't a solution either, since old women traveling alone to other parts of Tanzania are immediately suspected of having been cast out elsewhere as witches. In the traditional religious system, witches are public enemy number one, capable of harming or killing others, and need to be eliminated.

Yet surprisingly, most victims of Tanzania witch attacks were not widely thought of as witches within their communities before being attacked, even if some family members had suspicions. The conspiratorial nature of witch killings within families means criminal investigations by local authorities typically go nowhere. Tanzania's former President Mwinyi visited Meatu in 1987 to urge an end to the slayings, saying: "You are killing innocent women, some of them your own mothers, grandmothers or old people who have all along taken good care of you: how come they suddenly become witches?"[4] But these pleas fell on deaf ears in Meatu, and the witch killings go on.

Why are there so many witches in Meatu? These witch attacks are rooted in traditional Tanzanian religious beliefs, especially among the Sukuma ethnic group that dominates the area. Witch killings are far less common in non-Sukuma areas of western Tanzania, a strong hint that cultural beliefs do matter a lot.

But—and by now you should be expecting this—it's also a matter of economics. Tanzania is already among the world's poorest countries and Meatu one of its poorest districts. It lies in a semi-arid region not dissimilar from the difficult Sahelian landscapes of Chad or Darfur. Life is hard in Meatu even in better times, but in drought or flood years—which are distressingly common—the ground produces nothing. In 1998 and 1999, just before Ted started doing field research there, a severe famine struck Meatu, forcing tens of thousands of people from nearly half the district's villages to flee their homes in search of food and water. The brutal laws of home economics and survival make elderly women targets during such times.

A survey we conducted in sixty-seven Meatu villages shows that nearly all victims of witch attacks are older females, and most come from "poorer than average" households.[5] These desperately poor households—those with the least land, cattle, and assets like radios or bicycles—would be those facing the impossible and agonizing resource arithmetic of many mouths and little food.

These killings don't happen at random. Witch murders and attacks are overwhelmingly concentrated in years when bad weather and the resulting crop failure cause farm incomes to plummet. In normal rainfall years, a witch murder occurs in a village once every thirteen years on average. In years of drought or flood, that rate nearly doubles to one murder per village every seven years. In the merciless famine year of 1998, there were nearly three times as many witch murders as in 2000, when moderate rains nurtured farmers' fields. One old woman every seven years is a lot in a village of only four hundred households. It translates into a 2 in 1,000 chance each year that a woman over age fifty is killed or attacked as a witch—nearly four times Colombia's overall murder rate at the peak of the 1990s drug wars.[6] These sorts of patterns should make us wonder what other seemingly "cultural" or "religious" phenomena in the world are also the result of deeper economic factors, something we'll return to later in the chapter.

Witch killings are unfortunately not unique to Tanzania. Attacks follow a similar pattern in northern Ghana, where thousands of accused witches have been attacked or driven from their villages in the past decade, often following struggles over household resources. Witch killings of elderly women have also been documented in Kenya, Mozambique, Uganda, and Zimbabwe, in rural India—especially in Bihar, India's poorest state—and in Bolivia. Over four hundred accused witches have been killed since 1985 in South Africa's poor Northern Province.[7]

Like elderly women, young children are also a net drain

on a household's resources. While they may eventually help to put food on the table when they reach adulthood, the short-term needs for sustenance may also put pressure on households to sacrifice their youngest members. Our economic model of witch killing would predict that children would also be accused of sorcery and witchcraft, and indeed many children are beaten or abandoned today in Angola and the Congo based on such allegations.[8] Once again, the supernatural belief in witches seems grounded in economic necessity. The belief that these witch children are usurping the life force of others serves as an excuse for desperate families to do what would otherwise be unthinkable: abandon their own kids during grim economic times. Economic deprivation may even have had a hand in the Salem witch trials, which took place in one of the coldest and most economically trying years for the seventeenth-century Massachusetts colony.[9] If the young girls of Salem had had full stomachs, they might not have imagined so many witches lived among them—and their parents might not have believed them.

What, if anything, can be done about witch attacks? Hunting down and punishing witch killers is unlikely to work. To our surprise, in conversations with Tanzanians from all walks of life, we heard that local residents would strongly resist any attempts to save "witches." Most Tanzanians believe in witches, and whether or not it's true, they believe that killing them can save their communities from future misfortune. It won't help to pull out our charts and Powerpoint slides to explain the role played by economics in witch killings: these beliefs are powerfully alive in Tanzania and much of Africa.

Ted found this out first-hand during his 2001 Meatu

fieldwork. During survey data collection he was stunned by his interviewees' nonchalance when conversation turned to the local witch population. They certainly understood Ted's interest in the matter—in the eyes of Meatu's residents, if you want to understand their problems, you need to understand their witches. And there was no apparent shame on the part of local government officials that witch killers were going unpunished. In one particularly chilling interview, a village council leader pointed out the house down the road where a witch had been hacked to death the previous week.

If local government officials aren't going to do anything about witch killings, what else can be done? If these attacks on elderly women are mainly the result of a rational cost-benefit calculus, then the trade-off faced by witch killers needs to be altered. One direct possibility would be to provide elderly women with regular pensions, like Social Security. Grandmothers and aunts would thus be transformed from household economic liabilities into net assets that relatives should be eager to keep alive and healthy to keep the government checks coming in.

This is exactly the approach taken in South Africa's Northern Province, where the elderly women are certainly grateful for their monthly pensions, at least in part for their protection against local witch hunters. When the country instituted a generous pension program in the early 1990s that provided monthly income to the elderly, witch killings virtually disappeared.[10] Funding such old age pensions in Tanzania, and perhaps other countries, could protect Africa's poor and elderly women. This would be an effective, but also very costly way of ending witch killing in Tanzania, and it is unlikely that Tanzania, which is much poorer than South

Africa, could bear this financial burden. Per capita health spending in Tanzania is just under $10 a year, so any government old-age pension in Tanzania would likely be too small to really make a dent in the problem.

Yet even without pensions or other government or donor support, the Ulanga district in southern Tanzania seems to have solved its witch-killing problem. In Ulanga, witch accusations and witchcraft beliefs are as common as in Meatu, yet somehow witch killings are almost unheard of.[11] Life in Ulanga is just as harsh as in Meatu, so the same economic forces should drive families to the same desperate deeds. Why the difference?

The answer lies in the assistance of traditional healers, another local institution that isn't usually associated with rational cost-benefit analysis, who provide a rudimentary safety net for threatened elderly women. In Ulanga, several prominent traditional healers—often women themselves— take in local people accused of witchcraft, providing them with food and shelter. In the hungry season of 1990, up to forty people arrived per day at the camp of the largest healer.[12] In exchange, the healers publicly "cleanse" the women of any past witchcraft "sins" in a ceremony where the reformed witches' bodies are shaved completely and their bald heads smeared with an "antiwitchcraft" medicinal paste.

When the witch's penance is complete—and presumably the hard economic times have also eased up a bit—the women are allowed to return home in peace, publicly "cured" of their witchery. The women and their families, when they can afford to, make payments of gratitude to the traditional healers in return for their past services, money that presumably helps to pay for the food and lodging of the next wave of witch refugees. Once we strip away the ceremony and ritual,

145

the arrangement looks like a form of insurance, or a simple loan contract: the rich healers (there's good money in traditional medicine in Tanzania) support the poor and elderly in bad times, who then pay them back when their situations improve.

The South African and the southern Tanzanian approaches both provide a safety net for the old and vulnerable, but neither addresses the underlying problems of droughts, floods, and famines that put poor households in this caloric vise in the first place. To really solve the problem once and for all, we'd need to help the entire household through difficult times by improving insurance against the extreme weather events that poor agricultural communities face. This would provide farm households as a whole with better means of safeguarding their resources even in the worst years, so there won't be any need to get rid of grandma, auntie, or anyone else.

Religious Zealots—or Economic Gangsters?

Religious passions are blamed for some of the world's most spectacular acts of violence. Almost daily, we read about the car bombings and terrorism in the Middle East, but many lesser-known violent criminals claim to be doing the Lord's work. Despite injunctions against indiscriminate violence in all the world's sacred texts, every major religion has their own self-proclaimed holy warriors. Building on the lessons of Tanzania's witch hunters, we might ask whether their crimes are sometimes inspired more by their pocketbooks than their

---

prayer books. That is, are some religious zealots just economic gangsters in priestly disguise?

The Mungiki ("the united masses") is one such group of violent fanatics whose stated purpose is to return Kenya to the pure precolonial religion and tra-ditions of its ancestors. Christianity is a no-no for Mungiki, as are beer and the tight jeans that are pop-ular in Nairobi these days. They prefer the Kikuyu god *Ngai* to Jesus or Muhammad, and a return to older clothing and hairstyles, including the dreadlocks worn by Kenya's 1950s Mau Mau freedom fighters. Mungiki leaders publicly rail against the corrupt postcolonial political elite as yet another example of the toxic ef-fects of Western culture on indigenous Kenyan values.

More ominously, Mungiki advocate the traditional genital cutting of adolescent girls, also known as fe-male genital mutilation, to control female sexual "urges"— and they've been known to carry out the procedure by force if necessary. Mungiki are also thought to be re-sponsible for the waves of gruesome beheadings in Nairobi's sprawling slums in recent years. Dozens more were found dead in 2007 as we wrote this book, some with their hands, genitals, and other body parts hacked off to be used, Kenyans say, in secret Mungiki religious rituals. Were these shocking and mystifying mutila-tions meant to intimidate Nairobi's largely Christian and Westernized population into restoring the old ways, or a means of placating Mungiki's gods—or something else entirely?[13]

When Kenyan investigative reporters got inside

the Mungiki black box—as best they could with so violent and reclusive a group—the motivations turned out to be much less . . . spiritually inspired. In addition to their religious and cultural agendas, Mungiki's less-publicized activities included the intimidation of slum shopkeepers to pay protection money, and other cash-generating criminal activities. Most of their earnings came from extorting the owners and drivers of Nairobi's crowded minivan taxis, called *matatus*. As a result, the media and police figured out that Mungiki's seemingly senseless violence wasn't random at all: many victims were *matatu* owners or drivers who apparently had refused to pay up.

Mungiki's beheadings looked like the handiwork of al-Qaeda religious fanatics, but they had more to do with the *Godfather* movies than with God. Whether it's the mafia-like Mungiki in Kenya, opium-growing Taliban forces in Afghanistan, Colombia's cocaine-trafficking communist FARC guerrillas, or the diamond-smuggling RUF in Sierra Leone, many of the world's religious and political revolutionary groups have day jobs as economic gangsters.

The Need for Action: Rapid Conflict Prevention Support

Failing rains lead to myriad tragedies in Africa, including the persistent civil wars we covered in chapter 5 and now witch-hunts. But knowing that a root problem lies in the weather can also help us to figure out how to most effectively ease the blows struck by poverty on Africa. Since Africa's vulnerability to the weather gods stems from a reliance on agricultural production, large-scale industrial development that weans Africans from their dependence on the weather would be the best solution. This may happen someday, and in fact most foreign aid today goes into long-run investments like infrastructure projects or education that tries to help push this process along.

As welcome as this aid may be, it does little to deal with the short-run, weather-induced triggers of African civil wars and witch killing. It's the feast-or-famine nature of rain-fed African agriculture that sets off conflict. So rather than focusing on raising overall levels of income, foreign aid also needs to be timed to get the continent's poor through the lean seasons when the rains don't come. Prevent extreme poverty today to avert wars tomorrow.

To translate this insight into policy action, we think more foreign aid should explicitly play an insurance role for poor countries. We call this new type of aid Rapid Conflict Prevention Support (RCPS).[14] RCPS aid would kick in for countries experiencing temporary income drops, in much the same way that it's better to see a doctor when you start getting sick rather than waiting for the infection to spread. By the time you've got pneumonia, it's already too late.

The same idea holds for countries, and thanks to our research on droughts and violence in Africa, we can recognize the clear warning sign that a conflict "infection" is on its way. When the rains don't come, violence and war can't be far behind. A similar logic and insight can be applied to other shocks to African incomes, like commodity price collapses.[15] Rwanda relies heavily on coffee export earnings to provide for its people, so when the world price of coffee plummets, so do most Rwandans' incomes. In this way, a sudden drop in key commodity prices acts a lot like a drought, leading to an unexpected decline in income that leaves the population desperate and violence-prone.

Since sharp and unexpected income drops are the symptoms of conflict vulnerability, donors should time foreign aid to provide relief when these circumstances arise. And this is when RCPS aid would kick in. When underlying economic factors return to normal—for example, when the rains improve the following year, or world coffee prices rebound— RCPS aid could quickly be scaled back as the state's own revenues pick up.

And here (finally!) the data are on our side. We already have the statistics and know-how to make RCPS a reality. Donors can track rainfall and famine conditions through publicly available websites. In fact, a database very close to what you'd need to do this already exists.[16] Monitoring commodity prices is even easier—if we want to know where coffee prices are headed, we can simply look up coffee futures prices on the Chicago Board of Trade commodity website.

Regular insurance programs have some built-in problems. For instance, automobile insurance breeds reckless drivers who can pass the financial costs of their fender-benders onto insurance companies. Similarly, if donors in effect reward countries for having conflict-prone conditions, this could reduce those countries' efforts to ensure that these conditions never arise. In this way, poorly designed conflict insurance could also breed reckless farmers who are less motivated to make sure that their crops do well, knowing that they'll be covered either way. Likewise, a country's leaders may do too little to deal with threats to political stability if they figure out that foreign aid will ramp up in times of crisis. If rapid foreign aid relief was given out based on poor economic performance alone, it could spur some government leaders to get up to all manner of monkey business—cooking the national accounting books, pleading poverty, even *creating* poverty—to extract more aid dollars for themselves. Although this may sound far-fetched, it wouldn't be the first time politicians exploited their people's suffering for their own selfish ends.

The elegance of RCPS—in contrast to current famine relief programs—is that there's little that farmers or leaders can do to game the system. Rain falls from the sky independent of any human intervention. Making the rains come (or fail) is not a policy option for even the most omnipotent of dictators. The same might be said of global commodity prices, which are determined by supply and demand decisions made all over the globe and are largely out of the hands of policymakers in any single country. This is particularly true for the poorest African economies, whose output is often a tiny drop in the massive bucket of global production. So RCPS insurance wouldn't distort governments' incentives to adopt responsible public policies to keep their economic houses in order.

We don't think RCPS insurance could or should entirely replace traditional aid focused on investments in infrastructure and education. But given that the fruits of so much foreign assistance are currently destroyed by armed conflict, RCPS can be seen as a natural complement to these investment-based forms of assistance.

Once we recognize that a central element of Africa's economic mess stems from armed conflict and other forms of violence, we should further target RCPS toward those most willing and able to participate in armed violence, to keep them out of trouble. Unemployed and poor young men have traditionally filled the ranks of criminal gangs (like Mungiki

CHAPTER SIX

in Kenya) and armed rebel groups (as in Niger). Temporary public works job creation for the young and disaffected might cause them to think differently about the cost-benefit tradeoff of taking up arms in countries threatened with crisis.

A more ambitious approach, and one well-suited to reducing the scourge of witch killing, would provide rainfall insurance for all poor farming households, disbursing aid funds when the rains fail, to keep stomachs at least partly full until the next harvest season. If this food aid were earmarked for the elderly, it would turn them into valuable assets to be protected rather than disposed of as witches.

Making RCPS Work

If RCPS makes sense in theory, there would surely be some kinks to work out if and when it is implemented. Would the money sent to starving farmers somehow be stolen by the government along the way? Should assistance take the form of cash or food aid? There will inevitably be some amount of learning through doing. Yet some successful African rural insurance programs that share elements of the RCPS plan already exist, and their effectiveness gives us some confidence that our approach will work in the messy reality of rural Africa.

The best known of these provides drought assistance to farmers in Botswana. Drought is a frequent visitor to Botswana, as in much of the semiarid tropics. Starting in the 1970s, the government implemented its groundbreaking Drought Relief Program (DRP) to help its people cope in dry years.[17] The DRP consists of direct income support for rural households in these years, including both types of assistance proposed above: public works employment, as well as food aid for the most vulnerable farmers.

It's estimated that up to 60 percent of rural Botswanans received some DRP assistance during the severe mid-1980s drought. (To put that in perspective, Medicaid, the largest U.S. social program providing health care for poor families, covers only 13 percent of the population.) In those difficult years, DRP helped preserve social stability by keeping rural poverty and income inequality in check. But Botswana's government got its money's worth: the country hasn't had a single year of armed conflict since independence in the 1960s. Botswana has been Africa's economic superstar for the past forty years, and it's likely that the drought insurance played at least some role in this success story. (In fact, former Botswana President Quett Masire told Ted that he thought DRP was a critical explanation for Botswana's remarkable run of economic good times.)[18] These agricultural insurance programs are part of the social contract between the people of Botswana and their democratically elected government that helps preserve peace and prosperity in this one small corner of sub-Saharan Africa.

The devil is in the design details, and these will depend on the particular needs and governability of the recipient country. Botswana was hardly typical for Africa when it chose to implement the DRP. Its government was already more accountable and responsive than most governments today. In settings like Botswana or Tanzania (another recent African success story), where leaders are by and large honest and well-meaning, channeling RCPS funds through the government would probably be the most cost-effective approach to the rapid deployment of assistance.[19] But RCPS programs can directly address government weakness and corruption in designing the form of aid transfers. For instance, where most aid would be stolen outright by the government, nongovernmental organizations (NGOs) should play a larger role.

Other kinds of foreign aid already out there bear some resemblance to RCPS but they differ in fundamental ways.[20] Most obviously, post-conflict countries already do receive large amounts of humanitarian aid from groups like the International Rescue Committee and the Red Cross. Like RCPS, this humanitarian aid also serves as insurance. But—and this is crucial—humanitarian aid is provided by the international community *after* a conflict has broken out. At that point, the levees have already broken, so to speak, and the damage done. RCPS would instead identify countries at greatest risk of armed conflict and increase aid *before* any violence erupts. Where humanitarian assistance is life support to keep a dying patient alive, RCPS aid is preventive medicine.

Some International Monetary Fund lending can also serve as insurance for poor countries, at least in theory. These loan assistance programs include the Compensatory and Contingency Financing Facility (CCFF) and the newer Exogenous Shocks Facility. Neither of these bureaucratic-sounding sources of aid is currently linked directly to armed conflict risk measures, and historically the CCFF has rarely been used at all. Unfortunately, the Fund's stringent conditionality rules on when it can disburse its aid—it tries to avoid countries with weak macroeconomic performance records on things like inflation and budget deficits—also prevents some of Africa's most conflict-prone countries from receiving help.

Foreign aid's main goal is bolstering countries' long-run economic growth potential, but it's also often an instrument for serving donors' own geopolitical objectives, something we can't forget when we try to understand how aid is distributed in practice. These concerns notwithstanding, we still maintain that far too little aid today focuses on insuring against the risk of drought, with its follow-on risk of armed conflict and other forms of violence. RCPS is an economically sensible means of providing a bridge to a more stable political environment, and can help create the conditions where Africans themselves want to invest in their own countries' futures.

Violence in all its forms—from witch killing to warfare—is partially a product of Africa's economic desperation and volatility. Once they get started, civil conflicts can last for many years, even decades. They've claimed millions of lives and created failed-state havens for international criminals and terrorists. The civil wars in Liberia and Congo became cancers for whole regions. And witch killings—just one poignant illustration of violent crime borne of economic hardship—show no sign of disappearing in Tanzania. Before picking up the pieces from another humanitarian catastrophe, or burying another elderly "witch," why not try to use some basic economics to stop the violence before it starts?

Looking beyond the Violence: Chad's Future

Another possible solution might seem to be on the horizon: harnessing some African countries' own vast natural resources. Recent discoveries of petroleum deposits in Chad by an Exxon Mobil–led consortium have generated tremendous hope. These large reserves could easily provide wealth on a scale that would swamp the meager agricultural incomes of

Chad's farmers. If these funds are used effectively, the country could put an end to its decades of poverty and violence, and start laying the foundations for a brighter, more stable economic future. But if recent history is any guide, we shouldn't be too confident that the funds will really be used wisely.

Africa's history is littered with resource booms that never translated into generalized prosperity. Diamonds and oil didn't help Angolans, whose country was governed by corrupt rulers and torn apart by years of civil war. And Chad's leaders seems little better. To the extent that stealing parking spots in New York City really is correlated with stealing government funds, Chad is in for trouble; it had the third highest number of unpaid parking violations per diplomat and recently tied Bangladesh as the world's most corrupt country in Transparency International's Corruption Perception Index. If left to its own devices, the odds of Chad's national oil wealth being well-invested seem slim.

After the oil find in the 1990s, massive infrastructure investments were needed to extract Chad's oil and send it down a 650-mile pipeline to export, and private oil companies couldn't raise all of the necessary capital. This financing gap was filled by international donors, including the World Bank in 2000, which stepped in with the hopes that this newfound wealth could lift Chad's people out of poverty. Even without hearing of the wanton parking habits of Chad's diplomats, donor organizations were fully aware of the endemic corruption in Chad's government, so they laid out unusually strict aid conditions on the project.[21]

The financing was contingent on Chad agreeing to commit a large share—over 80 percent—of the eventual oil revenues toward poverty reduction programs under what the

World Bank called the "Revenue Management Project." In a novel arrangement for aid donors, these oil funds were to be deposited in a London bank account and monitored by an oversight board called the International Advisory Group (IAG). The IAG was composed of civil society groups and both local and international development experts, all of whom would follow the money trail. Ten percent of revenues were to be set aside in a "Future Generations" fund, also deposited in London, that would provide for a time when all the oil was gone. Donors made it very clear that the Chadian regime would be punished for any attempt to subvert the agreement. In theory at least, Chad's government, donors, and the IAG were going to be partners in the shared goal of economic development.

If good donor intentions—and resources—were enough, Chad would now be one of our African success stories rather than a poster child for economic failure. But it obviously didn't work out that way. Once the oil started to flow, the World Bank lost its leverage over Chad's government and its notoriously venal leader, Idriss Deby, himself a former rebel warlord. Deby suspended his cooperation with the IAG and the World Bank in late 2005, publicly humiliating then Bank president Paul Wolfowitz and making a mockery of his very public anticorruption crusade. Once the oil pipeline was up and running—and he had rewritten Chad's constitution to allow himself to serve indefinitely as president—Deby had little further need for donors and their pesky conditions, and with oil prices over $70 a barrel, he was rolling in money. As we write this, the revenue management program isn't dead—yet—but with oil now far above $100 a barrel, Deby has forced the donors to accept an even larger increase in the share of oil revenues under his own direct control.

Much of the oil windfall has probably been stolen, although it is impossible to say how much. Deby has opted to use much of the revenue to finance his army in its ongoing battles with rebels in the north and east of the country, and for the occasional border skirmish with the Nigerian army in the west. The refugee surge from the Darfur genocide has given Deby a convenient excuse to disregard the earlier agreements (although we must, with some reluctance, give Deby his due: some of the extra military spending may be justified, given the chaotic conditions prevailing near Darfur and the rebel threat). Meanwhile the country still has no electricity outside the capital city, and living conditions for everyday people are as desperate as ever.

No one can yet say whether the Chad oil pipeline will someday help reduce poverty in one of the world's poorest and most violent countries. It's still possible that oil revenues will provide a basis for future economic prosperity, and the World Bank loan will have been instrumental in reaching that brighter future. But since Chad's oil finally started flowing in 2003, corruption and conflict have continued to stand in the way of real progress. Reaching back to the foreign aid debate we discussed in chapter 1, poverty traps can't always be broken with money alone.

Chapter Seven

The Road Back from War

The Vietnam National Army Museum in Hanoi isn't your typical tourist destination. There aren't snack bars or fancy gift shops. Instead, in room after room the museum displays tons (literally) of guns, grenades, shells, and other armaments used by the Vietnamese and their recent war adversaries. The only sculpture is the twisted metal frame of a downed U.S. fighter plane. The museum commemorates Vietnam's proud military history: some of the world's mightiest armies—including those of the United States, China, Japan, and France—fought and lost wars in Vietnam during the twentieth century, a point the Vietnamese are eager to share with foreigners (especially American, Chinese, Japanese, and French ones).

During Ted's visit to the museum in 2005, one of the most crowded exhibits was a collection of bomb casings used by the U.S. military in the 1960s and 1970s, during what the

Vietnamese call "the American War." The bombs come in all shapes and sizes, from sleek red rockets that look like slightly overgrown children's toys to massive, shapeless black bunker busters that loom above browsing visitors. The display is housed in a tranquil flower-lined courtyard, a setting that stands in sharp contrast to the macabre focus of the exhibit. This ironic twist is not lost on the older Vietnamese visitors, who suffered through the deafening chaos, heartbreak, and destruction unleashed by these objects of war.

Many Vietnamese failed to survive to be able to browse among the war era bombs-turned-modern-art project in modern Hanoi. Precise war casualty estimates are hard to come by—the chaos of war doesn't lend itself to gathering accurate figures—but the Vietnamese government estimated that over five million Vietnamese died, a number just about equal to the population of the entire state of Colorado. Most were civilians.[1]

The United States outdid itself, and everyone else, in its aerial bombing of the Vietnamese countryside (hence the ready availability of bomb casings for the museum). In the densest bombing in history, U.S. bombers dumped more than two-hundred pounds of high explosives per Vietnamese citizen, more than the body weight of the entire Vietnamese nation. Even a pinch of the stuff would knock you out of the chair where you're sitting reading this book. The military historian Michael Clodfelter calculated that the 7.6 million tons of bombs the American armed forces dropped on Indochina (Vietnam, Laos, and Cambodia) was more than triple the tonnage of explosives in all of World War II in Europe and the Pacific combined, and fifteen times the tonnage the United States used in the Korean War.[2] Clodfelter estimated that the bombing campaign of the late 1960s destroyed 65 percent of North Vietnam's oil storage capacity, 59 percent of its power plants, and over half its major bridges. The United States destroyed some bridges multiple times, bombing and re-bombing after each Vietnamese rebuilding effort, leaving much work to be done to again make these areas fertile terrain for future commerce and investment. The bombing also turned millions of civilians into refugees, opening the possibility that such regions would remain stagnant if industrious citizens chose never to return. And that's not even counting the unexploded ordnance and leftover mines, the unwanted gift that keeps on giving.[3]

Any modern war leaves indescribable damage in its wake, including the destruction of physical capital (like roads and factories) and what we economists euphemistically term the loss of "human resources" (the death or maiming of skilled workers). As a result, a country's income and productivity is almost always depressed immediately following a war on its territory. And if there's a country where we would intuitively expect war's impacts to endure, it's Vietnam. At the start of the war in the 1960s, Vietnam was already one of the world's poorest countries. The devastation wrought by American bombs certainly had the potential to drive Vietnam into the type of deeply rooted poverty trap we've found in Chad and elsewhere in Africa. Yet Vietnam recovered. Why?

These same horrific conditions can create a lot of opportunities for profitable investments as rebuilding gets underway. Theoretically, entrepreneurs with the skills to identify and exploit these opportunities—and the courage to open businesses in a ruined economy—can bootstrap the country into a postwar economic boom. Investors make money, their reconstruction efforts boost employment, and the country is pulled back to where it would have been without the war. For example, the value of rebuilding a road that connects a rich farming region to a big city—linking farmers to markets, and providing urban factory workers and office clerks with cheap food—is huge. In an economy where even the most basic productive infrastructure has been destroyed, many more of these high return investments will present themselves.

This kind of rapid reconstruction is exactly what happened in Japan after the United States dropped atomic bombs on Hiroshima and Nagasaki in August 1945 to end World War II. The attacks inflicted massive damage. In Hiroshima, the blast leveled every building within a one-mile (1.6 kilometer) radius, liquefied asphalt, and killed 70,000 civilians instantly. By the end of 1945, 100,000 were dead from the radiation or injuries. Many more later suffered excruciating deaths from radiation exposure, and hundreds of thousands of burned and scarred victims were left homeless.[4]

Yet Columbia University economists Don Davis and David Weinstein found that these two cities, and others destroyed by the U.S. bombing of Japan during World War II, have done amazingly well since the war on the most basic dimension of economic viability, their populations.[5] Davis and Weinstein compare the cities destroyed by bombing to those untouched by war, like the ancient capital Kyoto, which was deliberately spared by U.S. war planners afraid that its destruction would rally nationalist resistance, and northern Japanese cities slightly out of U.S. bombers' range. Surprisingly, the populations of those cities that were bombed bounced back to pre–World War II population trends within only twenty-five years after the war.

Hiroshima and Nagasaki built their way out of the

rubble within twenty-five years too, and today are both populous and prospering. The same is true of Tokyo. While firebombing there destroyed forever some of its most elegant neighborhoods—most of Tokyo's traditional wood-constructed buildings burned uncontrollably during the attacks—they were replaced with modern apartment towers and are now some of the most expensive addresses in the world.

At least in theory, rapid postwar recovery is possible for poor countries just as it was for Japan. But things don't necessarily work out as we'd predict when economic theory meets the realities of a postwar society. In our stripped down description of the world—where people and machines unite to restore a country to its former glory as long as appropriate investments are made—we've ignored many of the other economic institutions that may be important in determining how quickly a country rebuilds itself. Corruption and lingering political violence carried out by economic gangsters may hamper postwar investment, as seems to have been the case in many African conflicts.

Politics itself may also be transformed by armed conflict. Wars can trigger broader political participation and social progress, as the country pulls together against a common adversary. The enfranchisement of the politically downtrodden— women, ethnic minorities, landless workers— has been a positive by-product of many wars, including in the United States: women got the right to vote after World War I, the African-American civil rights movement took off after World War II, and the turmoil of the Vietnam War era brought new student voices into U.S. politics and helped launch the modern feminist movement. These kinds of political changes can lead indirectly to greater investment in what economists call "public goods"—investments like education and health care for previously marginalized groups—that benefit society as a whole.

War itself can also spur technological innovation that boosts growth down the line. In World War II, clashes on the battlefield provoked a technological arms race, as the United States and Germany worked to design faster bombers and more accurate means of delivering their payloads. The resulting innovations led to faster commercial jets and laid the foundations of modern computer science, spurring even faster economic growth once war ended. You could think of Boeing's billion-dollar profits today as the distant economic echo of these earlier technological revolutions.

Investments, politics, technology: the long-run consequences of postwar reconstruction are the product of these various factors. But to sort out this jumble of explanations, we need data, and that's something war-torn economies usually fail to deliver. Yet while the U.S. military couldn't wipe out the Vietcong, they at least kept a remarkably detailed record of their attempts to do so, and this gives us the information we need to discover how Vietnam recovered from its American War. Unraveling this mystery should help us figure out how to help other war-torn countries bounce back after the violence ends.

Masters of War

During the war, U.S. pilots recorded details of every bombing run in mission logs, information that was ultimately reported back to the Joint Chiefs of Staff. As a result, the Defense Security Cooperation Agency housed at the National Archives contains information on all explosives dropped from U.S.

and allied airplanes and helicopters between 1965 and 1975, providing a complete account of the bombing of Vietnam. Why do we have such staggering data for this war when most other conflicts are data black holes? Maybe that's what happens when you put an economist in charge of running a war. Then Defense Secretary Robert McNamara—an economist who trained at the University of California, Berkeley, and Harvard, and who later became president of the World Bank—established this detailed data system to keep close tabs on the performance of his military machine.

Following the war, the United States handed the data over to the Vietnamese government, in part to help in their efforts to clear the country of land mines: the U.S. had laid millions of them, and the Joint Chiefs' dataset had the location of nearly each and every one. Indeed, the lists included the location and type for all explosives inflicted during the war—general-purpose bombs, cluster bombs, chemicals, rockets, missiles, projectiles, ammunition, mines, and flares—all the various and sundry shapes and sizes that are on display at the Hanoi Army Museum.

During ten years of war, an *average* of 83.7 bombs, missiles, and rockets were delivered per square mile nationwide. That's the equivalent of blasting the island of Manhattan—a mere 22.7 square miles—with nearly two thousand bombs, each containing hundreds of pounds of explosives. Imagine New York's Central Park as a moonscape pockmarked by twenty-foot craters and littered with tons of metal bomb debris, and you have a picture of much of postwar Vietnam.

But averages can be deceiving, as some areas took a bigger hit than others. Roughly 70 percent of all explosives were dropped on only 10 percent of the country's 584 government districts.[6] The heaviest bombing took place in Quang Tri, in

Figure 7.1: Quang Tri province—dots denote U.S. bombs dropped

the center of the country near the 17th parallel, the border between what was then North and South Vietnam. Some districts in Quang Tri were pounded by over 1,200 bombs per square mile (the equivalent of dumping over 27,000 bombs on Manhattan), amounting to hundreds of thousands of pounds of explosives. Less was left standing in parts of Quang Tri than in Hiroshima after the A-Bomb, and by the end of the war, only eleven of some 3,500 villages were left untouched by high explosives. The areas immediately to the north and south of Quang Tri were heavily damaged as bombs and artillery flew over the North-South Vietnam border in both directions.

Coastal North Vietnam and some districts of Hanoi were also brutalized by aerial attack, as was the region adjacent to Cambodia near Saigon in the south. This latter region was the route of North Vietnamese and Vietcong guerrilla incursions via the Ho Chi Minh Trail, a makeshift supply track that ran from North Vietnam through Laos and Cambodia before reentering South Vietnam. The North's major urban population centers were largely spared during the Johnson administration, but Nixon and his generals later approved a much broader set of targets, including civilian residential areas during the so-called "Christmas Bombing" of 1972.

As profoundly horrible as it must have been to experience, this singling out of specific areas for particularly heavy attack is crucial in figuring out the impact of different degrees of bombing intensity. It allows us to compare the postwar economic performance in areas that were intensively bombed to those that received lighter damage, something that wouldn't be possible if everyone had suffered the same damage as Quang Tri.

How did the bombing affect the Vietnamese economy? The government of Vietnam didn't collect any systematic economic data in the years right after the American War ended in 1975, so it's hard to say exactly how quickly Quang Tri and the rest of Vietnam recovered. But good census and household data, measuring things like family incomes and expenditures, began to appear in the early 1990s, so together with our colleague Gerard Roland we were able to trace out what was accomplished economically after about two decades of postwar reconstruction.

The bombed out regions bounced back with a vengeance. The intensity of the war's destruction is almost entirely unrelated to the fraction of Vietnamese living in poverty by 1999.

So just like Hiroshima and Nagasaki in Japan after World War II, areas devastated by bombing in Vietnam have completely caught up with their neighbors only twenty-five years after war's end.[7] This economic catch-up was probably both a cause and effect of the recovery in population densities in bombed-out districts. Returning refugees helped in the rebuilding, and as the economy recovered even more were attracted to the area by the local economic expansion. Beyond migration through voluntary individual choices, though, some of these large postwar population movements were also orchestrated by the North's victorious Communist government, through incentives or coercion.

Vietnam as a whole enjoyed a postwar economic boom and posted impressive gains in a range of indicators of economic progress. Before the war, in the early 1960s, Vietnam had relatively few schools, and not many outside the country's few cities had electrical power at home. But by 1999, 71 percent of households had access to electricity and 88 percent of adults were literate. Once again these rates are largely independent of the extent of war-era destruction. The Vietnamese invested heavily in both physical and human capital after the war, as basic economic growth theory would have predicted. Economic conditions in the areas that bore the brunt of the United States's assault are—miraculously—almost indistinguishable from other areas today.

17° North Latitude

American bombs don't "drop from the sky" in quite the same sense as the African rains described in chapter 5; they arrived by design, planned by the decidedly nonrandom strategic thinking of expert military planners like McNamara.

Why, for example, did Americans single out certain areas for particularly harsh treatment? Historian Earl Tilford argues that American generals partly modeled their aerial campaign in Vietnam on the strategic bombing raids of World War II, which were designed to knock out enemy industrial targets (such as the industrial cities of Hiroshima and Nagasaki in Japan), to "destroy North Vietnam's industries and wreck its transportation system, thereby preventing North Vietnam from supporting the insurgency in South Vietnam."[8]

Nagasaki had prospered because it had an excellent natural harbor that was a center for commerce and later for manufacturing. This had also made it a natural target for U.S. warplanes, and maybe in the absence of U.S. bombs Nagasaki would actually have been even richer than the rest of Japan today. Similarly, suppose the strategic targets that American generals selected for intense bombing in Vietnam were also the places that would potentially bring Vietnam's economy into the industrial age. Perhaps in the absence of the American War, they too would have been even richer than the areas around them, and it's only because of the pounding they took from U.S. bombers that they're no better off than the rest of Vietnam.

Yet some aspects of U.S. bombing were nearly random, or at least unrelated to future industrial potential. Quang Tri, in particular, didn't suffer at all for its industrial development. It had none. The region had the simple misfortune of sitting at exactly 17° latitude north of the equator, which was the arbitrary dividing line between North and South Vietnam. The placement of this border had no particular logic outside of the backroom Cold War negotiations that accompanied the 1954 division of Vietnam. The United States

wanted to push the border further north to expand its capitalist ally South Vietnam, while the Soviet Union pressed to
move it south to enlarge Communist North Vietnam. In its
efforts to reinforce this dividing line at 17°, the American air
war in Vietnam concentrated on the unlucky districts, like
Quang Tri, that happened to be close to the border.

So, being near the 17th parallel resulted in more bombs,
but it's unrelated to potential industrial development. If we
thought that more bombing hindered future economic development, then areas near Vietnam's Cold War border
should be poorer today than the rest of the country—but
they're not. Districts near the old border are booming, along
with the rest of Vietnam, despite having had the double misfortune of heavy bombing and also being farther away from
the country's two major urban markets of Hanoi and Ho Chi
Minh City.

The fact that the American War's economic impact
was so fleeting is of course welcome news, but it doesn't tell
us how places like Quang Tri could bounce back after such
widespread destruction. The government certainly played a
significant role, as it made rebuilding destroyed infrastructure a top priority. According to the government's own data,
the more heavily bombed provinces received twice as much
public investment as other provinces from 1976 to 1985.
This ratio increased further with the end of Vietnamese
army clashes with China and Cambodia in 1980, as peace
allowed the country to finally shift resources away from its
military. The leaders of postwar Vietnam were anything
but economic gangsters in their investment of public
funds.

The Vietnamese population also coped in ways that

made it easier for hard-hit areas to bounce back quickly. They developed ingenious approaches to minimize casualties during intense bombing, hiding for extended periods in the thousands of miles of well-provisioned underground tunnels that were built during the war. Most people who left battle zones later returned home to rebuild.

Promoting literacy was a central aim of the North Vietnamese regime, and they managed to carry out large scale school construction and literacy campaigns during the 1960s and 1970s, too, despite the war's chaos. Since school buildings were vulnerable to bombing, teachers and students often dispersed into small groups to avoid air strikes. Rather than playing outdoor ball games at recess like kids elsewhere, or gossiping about who was dating whom, Vietnamese students spent their spare time building foxholes. They always had to have their helmets at the ready for protection when U.S. bombers threatened overhead, which in some regions was a weekly or daily occurrence. The helmets had to be grabbed at a moment's notice, perhaps mid-lesson, as the students ran into bomb shelters outside.

Vietnam's rapid economic recovery can never erase the memories of the suffering and trauma that people in the worst hit regions experienced both during and after the war. There is much more to life than GDP. Heavily bombed provinces currently have higher rates of disabilities, probably from bombing, the defoliant chemical Agent Orange, and later land mine injuries. Millions died and millions more grieved for lost children, friends, relatives, neighbors, and spouses. But in strictly economic terms at least, the recovery has been stunning.

The Vietnam that might have been . . .

Our approach to estimating the war's economic effects allows us to understand differences across districts within Vietnam, but it can't really capture bombing's effects on the country as a whole. Despite the postwar recovery in heavily bombed regions, it's possible there were still adverse nationwide effects that touched all regions. And no matter how rapid the recovery, the war, in addition to all the direct pain and suffering the conflict wrought, was definitely a short-run economic disaster since so much time and energy was spent fighting rather than working at economically productive activities. Vietnam's southeast Asian neighbors—like the "Tiger economies" of Malaysia and Thailand—didn't suffer from the American War. Income per capita is now $4,970 in Malaysia and $2,720 in Thailand—but only $620 in Vietnam.[9]

Yet for all the suffering it caused, the war did have at least a hint of a silver lining for the Vietnamese people. The conflict generated a stronger sense of Vietnamese national identity, forged through shared struggles and sacrifice. In the long-run, this feeling of common purpose can help to foster peace, consensus, and political stability—and even indirectly boost economic growth.

But never mind the might-have-beens, positive or negative. Vietnam has enjoyed a postwar economic boom, and these benefits have extended to even its most war-ravaged areas. Since embarking on free market reforms in 1993, the Vietnamese economy has grown by more than 6 percent per year, faster than almost any other country on the planet. So any damage to long-run growth prospects from the war can't have been too great. Vietnamese per capita income is now twice as high as in most African countries, and the gap between them keeps growing.[10]

Vietnam didn't fall into a poverty trap despite the most intense bombing in history. Economic recovery from war is possible even for the poorest of the world's poor, provided economic gangsters don't get in the way.

Louder Than Bombs

Even with the unprecedented bombing they suffered, Japan and Vietnam did have a major advantage in their postwar recovery: they both emerged from struggles against foreign armies. As politicians have known since the time of Pericles, nothing rallies the troops like a common enemy. Fighting an outside force fans nationalist passions and unifies the population, and could very well have more positive than negative impacts on society and government institutions.[11]

Civil wars are likely to have the opposite effect, destroying unity and leaving behind deep social divisions. And most fighting in the world today takes place in the context of civil wars, not struggles against foreign armies. In Rwanda, neighbors killed neighbors, and in Sierra Leone armies of children were forced to attack their home villages, sometimes massacring their own parents. At war's end, these communities so divided by civil war are condemned to live together again. Resentments run deep, and in many cases postwar politics revolves around settling old scores rather than building a shared future.

The scars of civil conflict can take decades or centuries to heal, even in rich countries—just ask anyone from the American South how they feel about General Sherman and his scorched earth approach to breaking the South's will to fight. A glance at the map of 2004 presidential election results reveals that the U.S. Civil War is far from ancient history: the old Confederacy was painted a uniform Republican red, carrying George W. Bush to victory.[12] Even though party labels may change, some basic political and cultural divisions across U.S. regions have remained pretty stable for over 140 years.

Also, the very fact that we were able to conduct a detailed statistical analysis of Vietnam's economic recovery makes it, almost by definition, a success story: collecting reliable household surveys and censuses of the type required for the studies of bombing in Vietnam and Japan is a luxury that the poorest nations can rarely afford. Countries with good data are almost never basket cases. This may lead to what economists call "selection bias": countries where the economy and institutions have collapsed after wars (like Chad, Afghanistan, or Congo) lack reasonable data, so we don't get to study the persistence of war's negative effects, while we are able to study the success stories in greater detail. The postwar recoveries of Japan and Vietnam prove that rapid recovery is possible, but they could still be more the exception than the rule.

African Failures—and Successes

As we learned in earlier chapters, Africa is the world's most conflict-prone continent, and many of its countries—Chad, Somalia, Congo, and Sudan, to name just a few—have been trapped for decades in conflict and economic decline. Africa's violent legacy is unfortunately grounded in the civil

174

wars that we've just argued are most likely to result in long-term economic and political stagnation.

But the news coming out of sub-Saharan Africa these days isn't all bad. Many countries are in the process of making economic comebacks, despite the social traumas of civil war. There are probably as many successful postwar recoveries in Africa as failures. Both Mozambique and Uganda enjoyed Vietnam-style economic booms in the 1990s following the end of their civil wars (which, in Mozambique's case, was accompanied by an end to Communist rule). Sierra Leone and Angola followed suit after their civil wars ended in 2002, and some of these countries' vast diamond and oil wealth finally seems to be trickling down to feed the poor. Even Rwanda, the site of the 1994 genocide and earlier armed violence, has had economic growth of 5 percent over the past six years, providing hope that better times could be ahead.

What makes these countries and their recent histories different from Chad, which remains locked in an endless cycle of violence? For the answers to that question, you would have to choose from an embarrassment of riches—there are many candidate explanations, but little hard evidence yet to help to evaluate their relative importance.[13] Research has so far been more successful in figuring out how wars start than understanding how to make peace hold. Still, recent experience suggests that there are some intuitive principles that are crucial for keeping the peace at war's end.

First, get rid of the guns. If the rebel leadership remains at large with troops and weapons squirreled away in the jungle, a pause in the fighting is more likely to be a temporary lull than a clean break with the violent past. Disarmament is critical to securing peace.

Sierra Leone is a case in point. At the end of its civil war in 2002, United Nations and British troops quickly moved in and aggressively disarmed RUF rebel forces. Some RUF leaders were later imprisoned and charged with war crimes in a special tribunal, and peace got an unexpected boost from the 2003 death (apparently from natural causes) of the top rebel leader, Foday Sankoh. Just as violence spawns further violence, peace begets peace. Each passing year makes Sierra Leone more stable, as any guns stashed at war's end begin to rust, and former soldiers age, fall in love, marry, work, and move on with normal lives. Eventually their battle days will seem like hazy, distant nightmares.

In addition to dismantling the weapons of war, it is perhaps even more important to nurture the instruments of peace and social tranquility. A strong government to keep the peace, enforce the law, and crack down on nascent rebel movements is essential to maintaining stability and promoting economic development. As we've already learned in this book, not all regimes are benevolent—many are corrupt and abusive—but life under an imperfect yet stable government is still almost always preferable to the horrors of civil war for most civilians, who bear the brunt of the violence, dislocation, and suffering.

Sierra Leone again illustrates these principles at work. During the 1970s and 1980s, the country was ruled by Siaka Stevens, who left behind a legacy of rampant corruption, widespread smuggling of diamonds, and a run-down economy when he left office in 1985.[14] As with others that fill Africa's pantheon of crooked postindependence economic gangsters—Mobutu in Zaire, Idris Deby in Chad—Stevens set out to degrade the country's governing institutions, which he saw as a threat to his absolute power and ability to steal the country's wealth. If Stevens left Sierra Leone's government organizations in critical condition, the war pulled the plug. By the peak of the civil war in the late 1990s, the country approached anarchy, and served to exemplify the failure of the modern African nation-state.

The postwar U.N./U.K. mission recognized these failures and pushed to upgrade and strengthen Sierra Leone's government. The occupying force brought Sierra Leone's elected president back from exile in 2001 and assisted him in rebuilding a functioning state, to make sure economic gangsters like Stevens wouldn't again return to power. Democratic national elections were held for a new parliament, and representative local councils were reinstated (they had been abolished under Stevens), giving citizens a voice in local affairs and increasing the government's local public services capacity. The armed forces and police were also retrained and given a four-fold pay hike.[15] For the 2007 presidential elections, parties held competitive internal primaries, and there was even a vice-presidential debate—the first of its kind in Sierra Leonean history. Driven by a new wave of political energy and activism, especially among young voters, the opposition party won a fair poll and the ruling party peacefully stepped aside.[16]

The country's incipient economic revival matches its political transformation. Economic growth has chugged along at 7 percent per year, albeit starting from the abysmal living standards that prevailed at war's end. With the threat of new rebel attacks safely in the past, foreign investment is pouring in, particularly in the mining sector and much of it from China. But it's not just foreign money driving the recent growth spurt. The government has also created thousands of public works jobs for unemployed youths: repainting buildings and road medians, and maintaining public parks. Perhaps heeding some of the lessons of Botswana's successful drought relief program (described in chapter 6), and with war traumas still fresh, Sierra Leoneans are doing things differently this time.

Sierra Leone has quickly gone from the archetypical African basket case to a new success story, but progress is still tenuous. The war's scars haven't yet completely healed: it remains one of the world's poorest societies and may only be one drought year away from disaster and a redescent into chaos. But in the meantime, life continues to improve, and the partnership between Sierra Leone and international donors to keep the peace and bolster the government can hopefully keep it that way. Even the world's poorest and most violent countries can change in a few short years with a little luck and some enlightened reforms. Sierra Leone's economic expansion doesn't rival Japan or Vietnam's—at least not yet—but life free from war and starvation may be enough for its weary citizens right now.

Rebuilding Baghdad

Baghdad was jolted from its early morning slumber on March 20, 2003 by exploding Tomahawk missiles, signaling the beginning of Iraq's "American War." In the weeks that followed, a pounding by hundreds of millions of pounds of explosives brought a quick end to the conventional war. With much of the country's infrastructure in ruins, various U.S. agencies planned a major postwar rebuilding effort. A strong U.S. presence remained in Iraq, and promised to help with reconstruction and deal with any remaining pockets of resistance. Pundits pointed to Japan as a model for how Iraq's recovery would proceed.[17] Japan was laid to waste by World War II, but as we've learned, it soon became a functioning democracy with a booming economy. With a little time, many thought, Iraq would be too.

Yet this has clearly not been the outcome in Iraq. What went wrong? When you look closer, the Japan-Iraq analogy starts to break down. While the physical damage of war was much lighter in Iraq—the U.S. bombing of Baghdad was a finger prick compared to Hiroshima—the political differences and social scars run much deeper. In drawing comparisons to earlier conflicts, Iraq actually has much more in common with African civil wars like those in Chad than it does with the physical destruction of a socially harmonious Japan. Unlike 1940s Japan, modern Iraq has a history of armed violence among its ethnic and religious communities—the Kurds in the north, Sunnis in the center, and southern Shias, and yet other smaller groups. Iraqis lack the sense of common national identity that served to unite postwar populations in Vietnam and Japan. Bridging ethnic and religious divisions requires reforms of social relations, culture, and government institutions, and these are infinitely more complex than patching up bombed-out roads.

Keeping the peace in postwar Iraq presented a much greater challenge as a result, though perhaps no greater than that of Sierra Leone's brutalized society when its war ended in 2002. But Iraq, as it turned out, was no Sierra Leone, either.

There were important differences in Iraq's rebuilding efforts. For one thing, the war never really ended in Iraq. In Japan, after the two terrifying nuclear attacks, Emperor Hirohito officially surrendered and publicly called for full cooperation with the American occupiers. Japanese soldiers dutifully handed in their weapons and returned to

CHAPTER SEVEN

civilian life (much as Sierra Leone's rebels were forced to hand over their weapons to British commandos). The United States then incorporated Hirohito—heretofore a vilified archenemy—and most wartime leaders into the occupying regime. Preexisting Japanese government institutions were reformed through a new constitution but not uprooted. This proved to be much more effective than simply tearing down the government at its foundations, since it's extremely difficult to build up state institutions from scratch.

With the exception of a few high-profile war criminals, postwar policy in Nazi Germany and Fascist Italy wasn't all that different than in Japan. In all three cases of World War II reconstruction, U.S. occupiers largely took hold of the existing state and economic infrastructure that had produced formidable Axis fighting machines, and set them to work on peaceful tasks like manufacturing cars rather than tanks. Mass political purges weren't part of the transition to peace. Explicit reconciliation has also figured into postwar Sierra Leone politics. As part of the peace deal, the RUF rebels became a legal and registered political party—though they didn't win a single parliamentary seat in the democratic postwar elections. Chopping off thousands of civilians' hands didn't play well at the ballot box.

The two key governing institutions under Saddam Hussein were his military and the ruling Ba'ath Party, with its 1.5 million members. As in the Soviet Union, Party membership had been a precondition for leading positions in many spheres of life—including university professorships and even hospital jobs for doctors—but after May 2003 Ba'athists were explicitly prohibited from holding public employment. The Iraqi Army was disbanded soon after the U.S. military reached Baghdad and scores of government

180

leaders were imprisoned. The country's intellectual and political elite, many of whom just joined the Party to get a
pay raise, were disqualified from helping in the country's
reconstruction.

Yet far more dangerous was the dissolution of the Iraqi
Army. This left tens of thousands of heavily armed men,
whose only job qualifications were sniper training and bomb-
making, with nothing to do and no means of earning a living. Unfortunately for the U.S. military and civilians, Iraq's
newest economic gangsters soon found ways to keep themselves busy.

The United States created a vacuum where corruption
and violence have flourished, and old ethnic and religious
rivalries reemerged, killing off any hope of a speedy economic recovery. Without strong government institutions to
hold it together, Iraq seems to be flying apart much like
Chad. Even if the United States were to heed some of these
lessons now, might it be too late to easily put Iraq back together again?

Diamonds Are a Guerilla's Best Friend[20]

In 2002, most Angolans were getting by on less than a
dollar a day despite their country's rich deposits of oil
and diamonds. After decades of civil war, they were
poorer than they had been twenty-seven years earlier
upon independence. Then Jonas Savimbi, commander
of the UNITA rebel group, was killed in combat with
government forces, leaving the rebels in disarray. As

citizens poured into the streets of their capital Luanda to celebrate, the rebels' fall augured newfound prosperity as well as peace.

Not so, however, for the businessmen who had extracted Angola's diamonds amid the chaos of war. When news hit of Savimbi's death, investors dumped their shares in mining companies with large Angolan operations. Using an approach much like our study of Suharto's health scares (in chapter 2), economists Massimo Guidolin of the St. Louis Federal Reserve and Eliana La Ferrara at Bocconi University found that these companies' stock prices fell by an average of 12 percent within a matter of days.[18] Why was peace so bad for the diamond business? And can this finding help explain why some wars—especially in resource- rich developing countries like Angola, Chad, Sierra Leone, or Sudan—have been so persistent?

Guidolin and La Ferrara argue that the mining companies took a beating from investors because the fortunes they'd made from Angola's diamond mines relied on the treacherous conditions created by civil war. After Savimbi's death, while mining companies with Angolan investments saw their stock prices plunge, those without Angolan exposure appreciated in value. In other words, an end to conflict hurt the dominant diamond companies by knocking down barriers to entry for competitors. Most people, including nearly all of Ray's first-year MBA students, think that the key to business success is cheaply and efficiently producing something people want to buy. If this were the case, then war's end should have made Angolan miners and their shareholders much richer as production costs plummeted. But the effect of peace on diamond mining in Angola shows that more important than producing something well is doing it better than the competition—and the potential competition.

Wartime Angola was a very expensive place for diamond miners to operate because of the bombed-out roads, kidnappings, and other conflict-zone hazards. Running a mine often meant getting your hands dirty. Companies reportedly employed guns-for-hire like Executive Outcomes, a private army recruited from South Africa's disbanded apartheid-era special forces, to keep their operations safe from rebel attack. The cost of protecting one mine alone could run as high as $500,000 a month, as the Angola Peace Monitor reported in 2001.[19] And to keep mines safe from government meddling, paying bribes was the norm.

Not every CEO or shareholder is willing to set up a private army, or partner with a real-life Danny Archer, the mercenary played by Leonardo DiCaprio in the film *Blood Diamond* about Sierra Leone. But some know how to turn wartime adversity to their advantage. Firms like Mano River Resources, Diamond-Works, and Rex Diamond have operated mines in multiple African war zones over the years, despite the costs and hurdles that drive out everyone else. That is, war acted as a "barrier to entry" that kept other companies out and insiders' profits high. After 2002, peace in Angola presented an opportunity for many new companies to bid for lucrative mining licenses.

Guidolin and La Ferrara found that, in fact, most of the wartime-dominant companies kept their mining concessions, and some even expanded their Angolan operations at war's end. However, the mere presence of potential competitors helped the government to renegotiate its contracts from a position of newfound strength. With peace at hand, as many as six other diamond companies reportedly also vied for contracts. Among them was global megamerchant DeBeers, which had pulled out of Angola during the war.

A peacetime Angolan government could also afford newfound patience in its negotiations. Before, the government had faced a constant budget crunch, and in its desperation to obtain hard currency to purchase arms, was forced to accept unfavorable terms. Peace meant that diamond firms no longer got the same sweetheart deals. Royalty payments to the government for mining concessions jumped from $37.5 million in 2002 to nearly $110 million one year later, despite only a modest increase in the value of the diamonds extracted. Overall, the Angolan economy has taken off since the war's end, with income per capita rising by more than 20 percent between 2003 and 2005— proving once again that the poorest economies can quickly rebound from war. If the old diamond companies are suffering, the rest of the country isn't.

In the oil rush that has seized much of Africa in recent years, we may be witnessing another disconnect between economic prosperity and business profits. Some Western oil companies, whether inhibited by ethics or constrained by law, have shied away from working with the most unsavory African dictators. But such qualms haven't stopped the China National Petroleum Company (CNPC) from drilling in countries like Chad and Sudan. As long as Sudan's government remains a global pariah for its role in the Darfur genocide, the Chinese will face little competition there.

This means that CNPC, like Angola's wartime diamond miners, also has little incentive to work for peace in Darfur. Quite the opposite. There is a tragic mismatch between the humanitarian imperative to end wars and the business imperatives of incumbent firms to maintain entry barriers. No one has the data to know whether the executives of companies with Angolan mines deliberately helped to prolong the conflict, but it appears it would have been in their shareholders' interests to do so. Even though rapid economic development and poverty alleviation are possible once the shooting stops, companies with a taste for operating in war zones, or collaborating with corrupt governments, may want to keep things as they are—because that's what's good for profits.

Chapter Eight

Learning to Fight Economic Gangsters

"Haba na haba hujaza kibaba"
("Bit by bit, you fill up the jug")
—Traditional Swahili proverb

Crooked politicians and contractors have been siphoning off cash from road-building projects for as long as there have been roads—maybe even longer. Road construction requires materials, like sand and stones, and lots of manual labor, all purchased locally by contractors. The Tony Sopranos of the world have figured out that there's good money to be made by overinvoicing these contracts: double the budget for building supplies, buy some cheap concrete, and split the leftover cash with your cronies in the roads ministry.

Kenyans blame this age-old problem for the potholed, traffic-clogged streets in their capital, Nairobi. Only 14 percent of all Kenyan roads were paved in 2004, barely changed from the equally dismal 13 percent in 1990.[1] Many millions of dollars were stolen, and foreign donors are reluctant to pour further aid dollars into the fiscal black hole of Kenya's roads ministry—once bitten, twice shy. As a result of the dismal state of Kenya's transportation infrastructure, what should be an hour-long trip can extend into a sweaty day-long excursion. For businesses and truckers, this translates into lower profits and lost jobs. Kenya also has one of the world's highest rates of traffic fatalities, owing in part to the obstacle course of potholes and gullies in the country's highways.

Here's a development problem we'd really like to understand better and to get governments to do something about. But so far Kenya's highway contractors have proven to be more elusive research targets than Chinese smugglers. And herein lie the ups and downs of studying economic gangsters: the excitement of the search for unexpected answers bumping up against the frequent frustration at failing to make a research dent in some of the biggest—and seemingly simplest—problems in economic development, like how to build better roads.

We've already documented the kingly sums channeled to Suharto's friends and family in Indonesia using only the bets placed by investors on the Jakarta Stock Exchange; uncovered the hidden tracks of China's smugglers, and learned how governments can fight back using the economic incentives embedded in the tariff code; and, through the parking abuses of U.N. diplomats, found that corruption is at least in part a state of mind. We're also finding new ways to understand and prevent violence, through the insight that the dire living conditions of desperate people can turn them into calculating economic gangsters. Understanding the incentives behind economically motivated acts of violence helped us develop new schemes to break the cycle of violence and poverty by using aid to stop violence before it starts.

We've gained new insights in our efforts to understand corruption and violence in poor countries—but they're only footholds. And the work we've described in the book is part of a much larger effort by the broader community of development economists. We're still only beginning to understand what can be done about Kenya's crumbling roads and the many other legacies of the world's economic gangsters. There are a dizzying number of plausibly effective policies, but how can we figure out which ones will work in practice?

Basic economic principles, combined with some common sense, can help to guide us in recommending possible policies. We know that economic incentives matter, so a good starting point for corruption is to think about the carrots and sticks that motivate potentially corrupt officials. Would greater government financial transparency—perhaps through web postings of highway contract announcements and more details on the winning bids—help curtail kickbacks in Kenyan road building?

Or how about increasing the salaries of government officials to reduce bribe-taking? Consider a junior policeman in Kenya earning just $65 a month. At this low salary, he will inevitably be tempted to shake down passing motorists for bribes. And anyway, what's he got to lose if he gets caught, bribe in hand—a crummy job that pays him barely more than he'd earn working on the farm.

But double his police salary and he might think twice about taking a bribe. While a monthly salary of $130 isn't going to make him rich, it is enough to feed and clothe his family, and is more than double the income of the average Kenyan worker. That's the carrot side of the equation. Yet even if he's unmoved by ethical concerns, he'll also be persuaded by fear of losing what is now a relatively high-paying job. This leads us to the stick in the policeman's cost-benefit trade-off: if officials were motivated entirely by economic incentives and conscience played no role, higher government salaries would only be effective in deterring corruption if accompanied by a credible threat of punishment. But if he can double his salary and continue to shakedown motorists and business owners with impunity, a higher salary would only have the effect of further straining the government's budget.

The Kenyan government did in fact double police sala ries in 2004.[2] Many other countries, often on the advice of Western aid donors, have recently done the same, boosting civil servants' wages at least in part to deter corruption.[3] What has been the effect of these reforms? Some people think it's helped to reduce bribery, while others claim that Kenya now has equally corrupt, but somewhat richer, policemen. If the pay hike was successful, are the improvements the result of newly indulged consciences—or the fear of punishment? Unfortunately, we don't have definitive answers to any of these questions because we have yet to come up with insightful ways of studying the problem.

Focusing on economic incentives can also help us design sensible policies to promote peace in turbulent communities. Now that we've shown that harsh economic conditions can set off violence in Africa, we'd also like to find targeted investments that pay off in more lasting peace. Poor young men, as the first to take up arms, must be given the means to withstand drought and recession without turning to violence. Job training programs could give these young men marketable skills—as carpenters, tailors, or auto mechanics—and their higher incomes could help see them and their families through bad times. By boosting the economic returns for staying on the right side of the law, this "carrot" might then dramatically alter the cost-benefit calculation facing potential criminals or even rebels.

The economic logic is impeccable and it underlies the design of post–civil war peace-building programs in many countries. But since research hasn't yet been done to convincingly measure their impacts, the effectiveness of these reintegration training programs in building a more peaceful society—better able to withstand the frequent economic shocks that hit poor countries—remains the subject of vigorous debate in the humanitarian aid community.[4]

Many other unanswered research questions remain in the realms of corruption, violence, and economic development. We've learned that corruption is not just a matter of economic carrots and sticks—culture matters as well—but we still don't know how best to change culture and social norms. Through anticorruption *telenovelas* in Latin America, or anticorruption sermons by village pastors in Africa? Similarly, if cultural factors drive armed violence in some societies, could truth and reconciliation commissions like the one in South Africa be part of the solution?

We hope to get to some and maybe all of these matters in our next few decades as economics researchers. But the fact is, so far we've had to be opportunistic in our research, and this has defined to a large extent which questions we've tried to answer. We studied the value of political connections in Indonesia because we could measure these connections and were also blessed with an all-powerful strongman with failing health. We used rainfall to study civil wars in Africa because good satellite data allows us to cut through the tangled web of poverty and violence.

Will research on corruption, violence, and economic development remain a patchwork of facts and results that never fully coalesce into a coherent picture? Or is there some way to be more systematic in our economic investigations?

Doctors on Trial

Our colleagues in medicine aren't so hamstrung in their investigations. Medical researchers are constantly inventing new treatments to prolong and improve the human condition, and follow a well-established protocol for determining whether these innovations are truly effective. Before medical innovations can be put to widespread use in the general population, they are first evaluated using randomized clinical trials, as dictated in the United States by the Food and Drug Administration.

Suppose you want to test a new therapy to fight HIV/AIDS. The randomized clinical trial "cookbook" is straightforward:

- Collect information on the health status of a sample of people infected with HIV—things like their weight, white blood cell count, and other measures that should be affected by the treatment.
- Then randomly assign each patient in your sample to receive either the new therapy (the "treatment group") or a traditional AIDS treatment regimen (the "control group"). Randomizing patients into the two groups can be as simple as flipping a coin.
- Keep track of any subsequent changes in patients' health status in both the treatment and control groups.

That's all there is to it. To find out if your new HIV/AIDS therapy is more effective than earlier treatments, just look at the data on how healthy the two groups of patients are after a few months (or years) of treatment. If treatment group patients suffer fewer AIDS-related complications than those in the control group, white blood cell counts remain higher, and the treatment group is healthier on average, we know the new treatment is effective.

Could some other difference between treatment and control patients account for the difference? No—that's the beauty of random assignment. As long as there are enough subjects in the analysis to make the results meaningful statistically, any other difference between the two groups is, almost by definition, random (remember that being assigned to one group or the other is the result of a coin flip). So we can safely say that if treatment group patients are healthier, it's thanks to the beneficial effects of the new HIV/AIDS treatment regime.

Over the past fifty years, the use of randomized clinical trials has unleashed an explosion of new medical technologies. But this would never have been possible if medicine had continued in its old ways, with doctors basing treatment on their own individual experiences, their "feel" for a patient, or ancient remedies (such as bleeding people with leeches). Grateful people around the world are living longer and healthier lives as a result.[5]

A Random Walk to Knowledge in Busia

There isn't any conceptual reason why economists can't harness the power of randomization, by picking villagers—or even entire villages—to receive an economic treatment, and compare these changes to control villagers. Armed with these ideas, we hope economists can generate similar breakthroughs in tackling the challenge of global poverty.

Economists have in fact started taking the lessons of randomized trials to heart in recent years, following more or less the same rigorous methodology as our counterparts in the medical sciences, in *randomized program evaluations*.[6] One place to witness this new approach to economics research in action is the district of Busia in western Kenya. Busia is a region much like many others in rural Africa, where most people live as subsistence farmers growing corn (maize) and beans, and dream of migrating to Nairobi for jobs and opportunity. The economists working in Busia—led by Harvard economist Michael Kremer, and including Ted— are at the forefront of a growing movement to get better evidence on what works in development.

In collaboration with NGOs, and the Massachusetts Institute of Technology Jameel Poverty Action Lab,[7] the academic researchers working in Busia have already used randomized evaluations to show that providing antiparasitic drugs for intestinal worms—a major scourge affecting over 90 percent of Busia's kids—can boost children's school attendance and may have longer-term effects on students' health.[8] Just as medical researchers are confident that their new therapies are responsible for health improvements among their treatment group, we can be sure that antiparasitic drugs are responsible for higher rates of school attendance. Since the schools where students received deworming drugs were chosen at random, the treatment schools are no different on average from the control group—except for having received the antiparasitic drugs.[9]

While it's natural to focus on a success story like deworming drugs' impact on school attendance, randomized evaluations don't always produce positive results about program impacts. That's part of their brutal charm: they also provide the bleak, unwelcome truth when an antipoverty project isn't working. And information on failures is just as useful as successes, since it allows policymakers to shift funding away from the projects that don't work and toward expanding those that do.

In Busia, for every success there have been two or three development projects that didn't have any meaningful impacts. For example, given the scarcity of textbooks in Busia's schools, it seemed natural to expect that providing more books would produce better student test scores. It turns out, though, that students in classrooms randomly assigned to receive extra books didn't do any better on average than their counterparts in control schools. Maybe other educational expenditures like higher teacher salaries would be more effective, or maybe Kenyan school textbooks just aren't any good. Paul Glewwe and coauthors find that standard school texts are written at too high a level of difficulty for most rural Kenyan students, probably because they were written to cater to the needs of the high-achieving children of the country's Nairobi elite.[10] Whatever the reason, we've learned that resources need to be redirected away from programs like these that, however well-intentioned, don't have any impact.

Thanks to the work of economists in Busia and elsewhere, policymakers in poor countries are increasingly able to rely on hard evidence when deciding how to use their very scarce resources. We now *know* the benefits of antiparasitic drugs in improving school attendance in Busia, and as a result the Kenyan national government has included mass school-based deworming in its official school health plan for the country. Word has spread, and other African countries have expanded their own school deworming plans, including Ghana, where over four million schoolchildren received antiparasitic drugs in 2007 to commemorate fifty years of independence.[11]

Corruption Lotteries

Just as economics researchers in Busia have started to learn how best to educate Kenyan children, we can be similarly systematic in figuring which real-world policies work best in fighting economic gangsterism. We've learned the hard way in economic development that lots of ideas that make sense in theory don't translate into effective practice. To understand which tools work best in combating corruption and violence, we can turn to the same randomized evaluation approach that has established the efficacy of deworming and the ineffectiveness of textbooks in Kenya.

The program evaluation "cookbook" is pretty much the same for corruption as it is for any other project. First, collect good background data, then implement the new program in some group of randomly selected villages (or ports, or police stations), and finally, measure whether corruption goes up or down in the places randomly selected for anticorruption sermons, or where policemen get higher wages (so they have more to lose if caught taking bribes), or whatever else the new program entails.

Yet while applying randomization evaluation to study corruption is conceptually straightforward, there are twists at every turn. For instance, how can we collect data on corruption levels? We might be able to employ some of the ideas described in this book, and others we'll talk about below, to do exactly this.

Also, while it's uncontroversial to hand out textbooks in village schools, it's politically delicate, to say the least, to start playing around with policemen's wages or a nation's tariff rates—or the assignment of government highway contracts. But perhaps not impossible. Developing country governments implement anticorruption campaigns all the time, sometimes on their own and often with the encouragement of international aid donors, so we might be able to wait around for these to come along and try to document their effects. However, one further problem is that governments often make lots of policy changes all at once in an effort to tackle corruption and promote investment more broadly. This makes it hard to disentangle the impact of any single reform. So a government that decides to pay higher wages to bureaucrats may combine this reform with, say, greater legal scrutiny of highway contracts at the same time.

Even understanding a single reform is difficult, since we don't know what would have happened in the absence of the change. That is, we don't have a control group. Maybe corruption was already on the decline before the reform. Or maybe it was increasing. Maybe corruption levels fell because of the reform—or maybe they would have fallen anyway. Or maybe anticorruption programs are put in place precisely because government reformers detected a growing threat from rising corruption. In that case the trend in corruption could be *causing* the reforms—rather than the other way around.

These are exactly the conceptual difficulties that bring us back to the importance of using randomized trials. If countries ever want to understand whether their anticorruption efforts are amounting to anything, and if we as a global community want to build up a toolkit for what works in fighting corruption, some systematic experimentation must be an essential part of our efforts. This will necessarily involve—as it has in Busia for education and health evaluations—an allied effort of policymakers and researchers schooled in the fine art of randomized program evaluation.

This is no pie-in-the-sky aspiration: former World Bank president Paul Wolfowitz made fighting corruption his top priority during his brief (and turbulent) tenure, and his successor Robert Zoellick is continuing these efforts. The Bank could very effectively serve as the coordinator of randomized evaluations around the world, and other studies that require the close government-researcher collaboration we describe. In fact, they're already well on their way to doing so: the Busia evaluations mentioned above all received World Bank financial and political support, as have the anticorruption evaluations we describe next.

Gangsters vs. Accountants

What insights can randomized trials provide about how to root out corruption in road building? This was the rather ambitious goal of economist Ben Olken when he set out to take on Indonesian road contractors for his Ph.D. thesis.[12] Using World Bank money, over six hundred villages were given nearly $9,000 each to build a local road. To keep the local builders honest, some villages were informed that their road project would later be audited to ensure the funds were well spent. Others gave power to the people, holding "town hall"–style meetings to allow villagers to discuss and monitor local politicians' construction plans. Community involvement of this kind has been held up as a cure-all in development in recent years, especially for governance woes like corruption. It makes perfect sense, in theory, that if locals can watch over how their dollars are spent, fewer dollars will disappear. But then again, there's a big difference between knowing something *might* be true and finding that it *is* true out there in rural Indonesia.

Crucially, there was also a third set of Indonesian villages in Olken's study where nothing special was done at all about corruption. These villages serve as the control group to evaluate the effectiveness of both the outside auditors and the town hall meetings.

Because of the randomized assignment to the three groups, we know that any difference in stolen cash is actually the result of the audits or town hall meetings. But how can we measure how much money disappeared? We do know the amount that was disbursed to fund each project, so if we only knew how much the roads actually cost to build, then the difference between these two sums would tell us how much had "leaked out," most likely into the pockets of unscrupulous contractors and public officials.

To measure construction costs, Olken sent teams of experienced engineers to all six hundred villages to assess the quality of each road built. For example, by digging up road core samples, engineers can find out whether a road has been "watered down" by using cheap sand instead of expensive gravel. To illustrate, after the $9,000 had been transferred to build the village road, if Olken's engineers estimated that the road actually cost only $6,000, we can conclude that about $3,000 was misused or stolen, one third of the total.

How much road sanding and stealing was prevented by

audits, and how much by town hall meetings? Olken found that audits prevented a lot of theft: in the control villages, nearly 30 percent of road funds were stolen while in the villages where contractors were forewarned about audits this figure dropped below 20 percent. So the audits reduced theft by over a third.

The impact of the town hall meetings, however, did not speak well for the effectiveness of local participatory democracy: almost as much was stolen in the villages that held town hall meetings as in the villages where nothing was done at all. When deciding how much to steal, local Indonesian politicians and their contractor cronies are much more afraid of professional accountants from Jakarta than their own neighbors.

Insuring Africa's Harvests

Crop failure begets violence, whether in the form of nationwide civil war, the crime of witch killing, or armed robbery. In theory, the answer to this problem is simple: provide insurance against droughts and floods for the most vulnerable communities.

Botswana's success with its Drought Relief Program provides some guidance for how to translate this insight into practice, and served as inspiration for our Rapid Conflict Relief Support proposal (discussed in chapter 6). But Botswana doesn't represent the norm, at least for Africa: it's a stable and prosperous democracy in a region full of basket cases. Randomized trials can help us figure out whether crop insurance will work elsewhere on the continent.

This is the research objective of Xavier Gine of the World Bank and Dean Yang of the University of Michigan, who are studying a crop insurance program in Malawi, a country in southern Africa, like Botswana, but with little of Botswana's economic or political success. Working with local government partners, they offered farmers in a randomly chosen group of villages insurance against low rainfall. Just as in Olken's road-building project, other randomly chosen villages serve as the control group against which any gains can be measured.

How much more predictable will living standards be from year to year because of the insurance? Will households be better able to plant high-yielding—but volatile—cash crops now that insurance gives them extra peace of mind? Will this insurance reduce crime rates following the inevitable drought years? Hopefully we'll know in a few years as their results start to come in. Solid research on the effects of crop insurance can help policymakers determine if and how new programs, like our Rapid Conflict Prevention Support plan, will actually work when our crop insurance theories meet the realities of African droughts.

Hopefully the lessons that emerge from Malawi will also help us design better rural insurance programs and fight violence before it starts. But there remain many other unanswered questions in economic development that we raised in this chapter and earlier. Randomized evaluations are not a panacea, and some questions will probably never be amenable to these evaluation methods. For instance, it's not easy convincing finance ministers to randomly increase the salaries of some government employees and not others (though Ray has certainly tried). Even if ministers were lining up to participate in these evaluations, researchers have to carefully consider whether any potential risks to people's livelihoods are outweighed by the value of expanding the frontiers of knowledge. With any research experiment—medical, economic, or other—these ethical concerns warrant careful consideration.[13]

Some experiments are simply impossible. We'll never randomize pay raises to Congressmen to see if that keeps their hands out of the budgetary cookie jar. So for some issues we'll need to continue our hunt for answers about economic gangsters in "natural" economic settings, as we've done throughout this book.

Still, for many economic development issues—from corruption and violence, to agriculture, education, health, and beyond—randomized program evaluations can help us find our way forward, learning from rigorous research at each step. With luck, the randomized evaluation method will be as successful in reducing global poverty in the coming decades as it has already been at fighting disease over the past half century.

The Road to Nowhere?

To understand why randomized program evaluation is so critical for the future of development economics, it's useful to travel forty miles down the road from Busia—a bumpy two-lane highway, thanks to Kenya's disappearing road funds—to the farming hamlet of Sauri. In this community, which appears much like Busia from the roadside (as Ted found out during a 2007 visit), a different type of economic development experiment is taking place thanks to the efforts of Jeffrey Sachs, the most visible proponent of the poverty trap view of economic development (introduced in chapter 1).

Professor Sachs is no side-line academic commentator or

Monday morning quarterback. Beyond his theorizing, he has also set out himself to *prove* that communities can be hoisted out of their poverty traps with his Millennium Villages Project (MVP). A joint effort of the United Nations and Columbia University's Earth Institute, the MVP aims to create "model villages" where the latest in economic development thinking is applied, to show that even the worst-case African villages can escape from extreme poverty. The MVP is among the most high profile antipoverty programs in the world today, and its efforts are frequently reported upon by an international contingent of visiting journalists and policymakers.

Sauri was the very first Millennium village. Like folks in Busia and most Kenyans, Sauri's villagers struggle to make enough of a living growing corn to get their children educated, while fighting a perennial losing battle with malaria and HIV/AIDS. The MVP attacks all of these problems simultaneously with the hope of breaking residents out of the cycle of poverty once and for all. In 2004, first-rate health specialists, teachers, and agricultural experts began working with community leaders to design a comprehensive rural development plan for Sauri. The approach reminds many of what the World Bank used to call its "integrated rural development" programs back in the 1970s and 1980s.

Thanks to the MVP, the village now has a gleaming new health dispensary with a maternity ward on the way, and has cleaned up eighteen of the springs that provide residents with water, to reduce child diarrhea. The primary school's lunch program is partially funded by the MVP, and tons of fertilizer have been handed out to local farmers to boost their corn crop yields.

At last count (in late 2007) there were already seventy-nine Millennium Villages like Sauri throughout Africa sponsored through massive private fundraising efforts with Western corporations and foundations, totaling over one hundred million U.S. dollars. Each MVP village receives roughly $300,000 per year over five years in external funding. This works out to about six hundred dollars per year for each of Sauri's five thousand residents, or nearly double the average villager's earnings in pre-MVP days. Sauri's promoters claim that their approach will prove to be revolutionary. Sauri "is a village that's going to make history," Sachs proclaimed in his MTV documentary, "it's a village that's going to end extreme poverty."

That was in 2004. What's happened since? The first year of the program was heralded in the global media as an enormous success: project reports tell of huge primary school test score improvements due to the school lunches, and a three-fold increase in corn production between 2004 and 2005 as a result of agricultural assistance.[14] Indeed, a three-fold increase in agricultural production would dramatically reduce poverty anywhere, and is cause for excitement. Perhaps the Sauri approach of air lifting in aid dollars for a few years—for fertilizer, health, and schooling—is enough to break rural Africans out of their centuries old poverty trap, and can generate crucial evidence in our search for solutions to global poverty.

However, before the project is scaled up and adopted elsewhere, we want to be sure that the MVP interventions are actually behind the potentially extraordinary changes taking place in Sauri. Suppose we find that Sauri's incomes are five times higher than today when we return to the village a few years from now, after all the aid workers have packed up and moved on to the next set of MVP villages.

Then we wouldn't need a carefully controlled randomized evaluation to be convinced that their poverty trap had been broken and something extraordinary was afoot—just as we wouldn't need a randomized trial to figure out that a new HIV/AIDS drug worked if none of the HIV-positive patients taking it ever got sick.

But suppose more realistically that the long-run economic improvements in Sauri are more modest—a 30 percent rise in incomes, say, rather than a five-fold increase. A 30 percent gain would still make Sauri one of the fastest growing areas in Kenya, but figuring out the MVP's role in raising incomes becomes much more complicated.

Is it because Sauri is somehow different from the surrounding villages, and that's exactly why it was chosen to be the MVP's model village in the first place? We might wonder if 30 percent income growth is large enough to justify the huge upfront expense of the program, in other words, if the program is cost-effective relative to other development programs. Were there specific components of the MVP program— say, the free crop fertilizer—that were particularly significant contributors to Sauri's success, while other components weren't useful at all? Without a serious program evaluation, we can't answer these questions with any confidence.

Unfortunately, a randomized evaluation is not taking place in Sauri, so as a result we really don't know how much of the tripling in corn production—or any other changes— can be attributed to the MVP interventions.[15] The early years of the MVP in Sauri happened to coincide with a national economic boom throughout Kenya. While still slow when compared to the recent double-digit annual growth in China's turbocharged economy, Kenya's 5 to 6 percent annual growth rate from 2004 to 2007 put it in the same league as some of the Asian economic tigers we hope Africa will someday emulate.

You could see the fruits of Kenya's newfound wealth all over Nairobi and other towns: cell phone salesmen sprouting like weeds in the concrete, imported Japanese cars clogging city streets at rush hour, and new condo developments racing to keep up with the demands of a nation suddenly on the move. Living standards were improving and poverty falling all over Kenya in recent years. Without a good control group of villages, it's impossible to tell how much of the economic progress in Sauri we should attribute to the MVP and how much to general economic improvements around the country.

Intuitively, it just doesn't seem right to attribute all the economic progress in Sauri to the MVP alone when economic conditions are improving more generally in Kenya. Similarly, if Kenya had experienced an economic slowdown between 2004 and 2007, it wouldn't be fair to blame any drops in Sauri's living standards on the MVP. In fact, as we write this book, Kenya has been hit by jarring ethnic violence following a contested national presidential election, and it could take Kenyan economic growth and investment years to recover from the resulting political instability. If Sauri's incomes fall as a result of this national turmoil, it clearly isn't the MVP's fault.

What of the three-fold increase in corn production in Sauri specifically? As we learned in earlier chapters, African farmers literally live and die by the weather. Crop failure and poverty lurk just around the corner whenever the rains disappoint—as they did in 2004, with precipitation levels 253 mm below the local rainfall average for 1998 to 2003.[16] With better rains returning in 2005,[17] there was naturally a recovery in agricultural production. It looks like Sauri's farmers should probably be thankful to the weather gods as well as the MVP's agricultural experts for their increased corn production between 2004 and 2005.

We genuinely hope that the Sauri model proves to be the great innovation that solves the problem of global poverty—and settles the Sachs-Easterly debate on foreign aid (from chapter 1) once and for all. But a serious program evaluation is needed to understand how and why its successes did (or did not) take place. Otherwise, we'll have learned little, and Sauri and the other Millennium Villages will likely join the long list of well-intentioned but ultimately inconclusive (and quickly forgotten) attempts to make poverty history.

Epilogue

Doing Better this Time

"Wisdom is better than weapons of war."
—Ecclesiastes 9:18

What Will the Future Hold?

We come full circle to where we started this book. Forty years ago, people throughout the developing world contemplated their futures with a sense of hope and anticipation. Since then there have been countries that have made the great leap forward to prosperity—South Korea, Malaysia, Taiwan, and now China. India may be next. But we've found that in all too many parts of the world, people in the village and increasingly cities—are scarcely better off than their grandparents were half a century ago. Poverty in Africa and parts of Asia seems more deeply rooted than ever. We've tried to understand how corruption and violence and their allies, the world's economic gangsters, get in the way of economic progress and what can be done about it.

Despite these deferred aspirations, hope has been rekindled—and not just in the commodity exporters, like Nigeria, that have benefited from the current rise in world oil prices. In recent years, Africa's new economic stars like Ghana, Mozambique, and Uganda have pulled off sustained annual growth rates of 5 or 6 percent per year, hinting at the promise of better days ahead. Even earlier disappointments like Tanzania may be breaking out of their economic malaise. These countries are full of dedicated and daring individuals struggling to steer their countries' economic and political ships in the right direction. In many cases, though, they are still sailing into a strong headwind of violence and corruption.

Ray had the privilege of meeting one such inspirational figure a couple of years ago at Oxford University. Kenyan journalist John Githongo's outward appearance was in every way the scholar, with the same understated manner and casual dress as the professors dining beside them at Saint Anthony's College. But rather than serving as a mere observer of society (like us), Githongo is part of Kenya's history in the making. In early 2003, when a new democratically elected administration took office, Githongo left his job as an investigative journalist covering political misconduct to become the government's head of ethics and governance, charged with rooting out corruption from within.

But the new Kenyan president's commitment to genuine reform—and Githongo's job—was short-lived. After a year or so, Githongo started to catch wind of the same shady deals he had fought as a reporter. The same transfers of public funds to non-existent companies. The same overpriced contracts. Mild manner notwithstanding, Githongo was not shy in speaking up about this return to the bad old ways, especially in a government that had just come to power on an anti-corruption platform. As he began to probe further— that is, simply to do his job—he was told to back off by senior ministers. Facing threats of unspecified violence against him and his family, Githongo was chased into exile in England less than two years after taking up his post.

Ray found himself sharing his recent research findings with Githongo in the surroundings where Kenya's leading anti-corruption crusader now wages his battles from afar. Githongo had brought his ammunition to Oxford for this fight, a detailed dossier documenting Kenyan cabinet ministers' admissions of their roles in concealing phony contracts that brought them hundreds of millions of stolen state funds.

It was surprising—maybe even shocking—that Githongo was neither bitter about his past nor defeatist about the future. His efforts had brought high-level Kenyan corruption into the spotlight both at home and abroad, and he had no intention of living out his days in some quiet ivory tower exile. Githongo was already planning to go back to Kenya, and spent his time at Oxford thinking about exactly what he needed to do upon his return.

Githongo and countless others have put their lives on the line—literally—to pull their countries out of poverty, and it's through their efforts that real progress will come to Kenya and other desperately poor countries. The two of us are researchers, not politicians or daring activists like John Githongo. But we too have a role to play in the global struggle against economic gangsters. We are the providers of information, new ideas, hard evidence, and maybe even some wisdom. Without the weapon of knowledge in hand, the John Githongos of the world will have a much harder time knowing how best to wage their own battles against corruption, violence, and the poverty of nations. We development economists are making our way forward, step by step, and hope our research can give the world's poor billions some inspiration and ammunition in their struggle.

Acknowledgments

This is an imperfect and incomplete attempt to acknowledge those who have made this book, and the research that underlies it, a reality.

We'd first like to thank our superb editors at Princeton University Press, Tim Sullivan and Seth Ditchik, who provided insightful advice, guidance, and support throughout the writing process, and tirelessly read and re-read (and re-read) the manuscript. Their intellectual fingerprints are scattered throughout the final product. Dale Cotton provided excellent copy editing, and the entire Press did a fantastic job in producing the book.

We are supremely grateful to our California colleagues Pierre-Olivier Gourinchas, Chad Jones, Shachar Kariv, Pete Klenow, David Levine, Enrico Moretti, and Dan Posner who carefully read through the book and attended our Economic Gangsters "mini-conference" at U.C. Berkeley in December 2007 that led to major improvements in the structure of the manuscript. Abhijit Banerjee, Stefano DellaVigna, John Dykema, Todd Fitch, Rachel Glennerster, Ellie Grossman, Dean Karlan, Ulrike Malmendier, Jamie McCasland, Jonathan Morduch, Dan Nguyen-Tan, Alison Reed, Gerard Roland, Adam Sacarny, Laura Safdie, Sarath Sanga, Shanker

Satyanath, Melanie Wasserman, Lauren Weber, and Stephanie Yee also closely read chapters, and we benefited tremendously from their reactions, perspectives, and suggestions. Peter Passell's excellent editing was instrumental in shaping chapters 4 and 7.

We benefited from superb research assistance from Jenny Aker, Alicia Bannon, Elizabeth Beasley, Lorenzo Casaburi, Bub Cathcart, Melissa Gonzalez-Brenes, Joan Hamory, Dan Hartley, Andre Heng, Jonas Hjort, Chang Hong, Pam Jakiela, Stephanie Jayne, Melissa Knox, Giovanni Mastrobuoni, Carol Nekesa, Avery Ouellette, Camille Pannu, Rachel Polimeni, Jerzy T. Rozanski, Adam Sacarny, Sarath Sanga, Monika Shah, Flora Shillingi, Valentine Shipula, Peter Wafula, Zhi Wang, Polycarp Waswa, and Yi Wu in writing the articles underlying this book.

The research would not have been possible without generous financial support from the U.S. National Science Foundation, National Institutes of Health, the World Bank, the Sloan Foundation, the Harry F. Guggenheim Foundation, International Child Support (ICS), the Meatu Tanzania District Council, Columbia Business School, and the U.C. Berkeley Committee on Research and Center for Health Research.

Ray would like to thank his co-authors on the papers that provide this book's foundation, and especially Shang-Jin Wei for his long-time collaboration, Ray Horton for guidance and mentoring, and Tarun Khanna for helping a lost and aimless graduate student find his way. Ray is also grateful to his colleagues at the Columbia Business School Economics and

Finance division and in the Social Enterprise Program for endless conversations on why the world is so darn corrupt. Ray thanks his parents, Michael and Sandra, for their unconditional love, support, and editorial guidance. And finally, Ellie, for her patience and love for an absent-minded professor.

Ted is grateful to his co-authors Shanker Satyanath, Ernest Sergenti, John Dykema, Gerard Roland, John Bellows, Rachel Glennerster, and especially Michael Kremer, for his inspiration and guidance. Ted would like to thank his colleagues in the Berkeley Economics Department for believing in the research; friends at Princeton University's Center for Health and Wellbeing, where some of the research was written during 2002–2003; and Stanford University's Center for International Development, where the book finally came together in 2007. Finally, Ted could never have written this book without the love of wife Ali, to whom he dedicates this book, or without the support of his parents Krystyna and Eduardo, or without the example of his uncle Adolfo Cuti nella in Montevideo, who has devoted his life to bringing clean water to people everywhere.

Notes

CHAPTER 1: FIGHTING FOR ECONOMIC DEVELOPMENT

1. Ngũgĩ wa Thiong'o (1967). *A Grain of Wheat* (London: Heinemann), 1967.

2. Lynne Duke, "Kenyan novelist Ngugi wa Thiong'o writes truth to power, speaking a language it can understand. Trouble is, sometimes power answers back." *Washington Post*, Sunday, September 17, 2006, p. D01.

3. "The outsider," *The Guardian* (UK), January 28, 2006.

4. See, for example, Luciano Iorizzo, *Al Capone: A Biography* (2003) (Westport, CT: Greenwood Press), Note that some of Capone's biographers dispute this widely held view of his early, legitimate career.

5. Robert Schoenberg (1992). *Mr. Capone: The Real and Complete Story of Al Capone* (New York: HarperCollins).

6. As we learned when we had nearly completed this book, the term "economic gangster" has already been around for at least a couple of decades. In particular, when the Japanese mob, or *yakuza*, came into big money in the 1980s real estate bubble, this new class of monied criminal was dubbed *keizai yakuza*, or "economic gangster."

7. Shaohua Chen and Martin Ravallion (2007). "Absolute poverty measures for the developing world, 1981–2004," *Proceedings of the National Academy of Sciences*, October 23, 2007, 104(43), pp. 16757–62.

8. This is the public slogan of the ONE Campaign Against Global Poverty (www.one.org).

9. Jeffrey Sachs (2005). *The End of Poverty: Economic Possibilities*

for Our Time (New York: Penguin). A related recent contribution is Paul Collier's 2007 book *The Bottom Billion: Why the Poorest Countries are Failing and What Can be Done about It* (New York: Oxford University Press). Like Sachs, Collier believes poverty traps are central to understanding global poverty, but is less optimistic about the effectiveness of foreign aid alone in tackling the problem.

10. William Easterly (2006). *The White Man's Burden: Why the West's Efforts to Aid the Rest Have Done So Much Ill and So Little Good* (New York: Penguin).

11. See the Transparency International website: www. Transparency.org.

12. Actually, this isn't entirely true. Germany, the Netherlands, Switzerland—nations with very low tolerance for corruption on their own soil—and many other countries used to allow their companies to pay bribes, just as long as it was paid to an official in some other country. Not only was it permitted, it was tax deductible as a business expense. As a result, multinational corporations based in these countries would regularly report large bribe payments in tax returns. This practice largely came to an end with the passage of national laws related the 1997 OECD Anti-Bribery Convention (see http://www.oecd.org/document/21/0,3343,en_2649_34859_2017813_1_1_1_1,00.html for more information (last visited March 23, 2008). As corruption researchers, we would love to find out whether it cost more to pay off the labor inspector in, say, Indonesia versus Bangladesh. Unfortunately, particularly now that such payments are illegal, we haven't had much luck in convincing companies to hand out this information. Besides, we should worry about the figures they were reporting earlier when the practice was legal at home. Since bribes were tax deductible before the legal change, companies actually had an incentive to *overstate* bribes paid to lower their taxes.

13. From a monologue by Gladwell at the TED 2004 conference in Monterrey, California. See http://www.ted.com/index .php/talks/view/id/20 to view the video (last visited March 23, 2008).

216

NOTES

Chapter 2: Suharto, Inc.

1. See "Suharto Son, Now a Fugitive, Flamboyantly Evades
Capture," *New York Times*, November 13, 2000.
2. Adam Bellow (2003). *In Praise of Nepotism: A Natural History* (New York: Doubleday).
3. Markets aren't always quite so perfect as in the idealized
description we provide here. Investors sometimes react too much
to news, and sometimes too little. In one example, the *New York
Times* reported the results of recent a breakthrough in cancer research on May 3, 1998. The company that owned the new technology, EntreMed, immediately saw its stock price jump from $12
to $52 a share, a more than four-fold increase. But the story wasn't
new news: the findings reported in the *Times* had appeared five
months earlier in the leading scientific journal, *Nature*, yet EntreMed's price had barely budged. So it would seem that investors
underreacted to the report in *Nature*. Furthermore, EntreMed
stock's highs following the *Times* story were short-lived. Within a
few weeks, its price fell to around $30 a share, suggesting that the
euphoric initial response was an overreaction. See "Contagious
Speculation and a Cure for Cancer: A Non-Event that Made
Stock Prices Soar," by Gur Huberman and Tomer Regev, *Journal of
Finance* (2001) for further details.
4. The value of futures of the Standard and Poors 500 Index—
a measure of what investors expected to happen to stock values
the next morning—jumped by over 1 percent at around 2 a.m. on
election night in 2000 when Bush was declared the winner in
Florida, only to drop back down a couple of hours later when the
Florida outcome was rescinded. Refer to "Partisan Impacts on the
Economy: Evidence from Prediction Markets and Close Elections,"
by Erik Snowberg, Justin Wolfers, and Eric Zitzewitz in the *Quarterly Journal of Economics* (2007) for details.
5. "Health matters for Suharto's children," *Financial Times*,
January 3, 1998.
6. A question that we often get when discussing these results
is whether we personally profited in some way from our interest in

217

the stock market reaction to Suharto's health. As investors without any inside knowledge, we could only observe Suharto's changing health status along with everyone else in Jakarta. For example, to profit from the news of Suharto's Germany trip, we would have needed this information before other investors. We could then have traded our shares in well-connected companies for those without connections before anyone else. However, by the time we got wind of anything, investors with much better information on Suharto had done their buying and selling, and market prices had already adjusted accordingly. Those wishing to profit from this sort of political trading strategy would have done well by cultivating links to, say, Suharto's cardiologist.

7. Where does the 25 percent number come from? To get to a full value of connections, we need to figure out how serious his bouts of illness were, relative to death. Specifically, what was the probability that Suharto was going to die in each of these cases? Suppose that the rumor of stroke meant that there was a 10 percent chance of death and resulted in well-connected companies falling by 2 percent. Then in some sense death (100 percent chance of death) would be ten times more serious than the stroke rumor, so we might expect ten times the effect on the value of well-connected companies—in this example, we would conclude that connections were worth 20 percent (10×2 percent). Without access to Suharto's medical charts, how can we figure out whether the stroke rumor meant a 10 percent chance of death, or 20 percent, or something else entirely? To make this admittedly morbid calculation we once again turn to the collective expertise of Indonesia's investors (who may well have access to Suharto's full medical history through secret conversations with his doctors). These investors were understandably worried about the country's stability in the absence of Suharto's guiding hand, and as a result of these concerns the Jakarta Stock Exchange Index (JSX) took a nosedive every time the president grew ill. This included a drop of about 3 percent when Suharto went to see his German doctors. Ray was fortunate enough to be living in Jakarta in mid-1996, and spent a few days wandering around the Jakarta Stock Exchange building asking investment bankers how much they thought the

JSX would fall if Suharto were to die suddenly. The consensus was "around 20 percent." So, one way to think about the trip to Germany is that it represented about a 15 percent chance of death (3 percent ÷ 20 percent). During this trip to Germany, well-connected companies dropped by about 3.8 percent relative to unconnected companies, so in response to Suharto's *actual* death we might have expected connected companies to fall by about 25 percent (3.8 ÷ 15 percent) relative to companies without connections. These estimates rely on a statistical technique called linear regression that we'll use again later in the book.

8. The widely used Polity IV database gave Indonesia a democracy rating of zero on a zero-to-ten scale for every year of the Suharto regime.

9. Perhaps not surprisingly, when change did come, it was brought about by popular uprising, violent protest, and rioting in the streets that ultimately forced President Suharto to step down.

10. "Politics, legal systems and corruption in Indonesia: A historical overview." INSEAD teaching note, 2002.

11. "Bribes, Extortion a Way of Life for Many in Sicily," *Associated Press*, August 15, 1992.

12. Economists Andrei Shleifer and Robert Vishny were the first to note the benefits of centralized corruption in the aptly titled article, "Corruption," *Quarterly Journal of Economics*, 1993.

13. See Mara Faccio, "Politically Connected Firms," *American Economic Review*, 96(1), March 2006, pp. 369–86.

14. See Don Wolfernsberger, "Punishing Disorderly Behavior in Congress: The First Century," mimeo, the Woodrow Wilson Center, 2006.

15. One recent exception might be the $90,000 of aluminum foil-wrapped cash recently found in the freezer of Louisiana Representative Bill Jefferson.

16. Seema Jayachandran, "The Jeffords Effect," *Journal of Law and Economics*, 49(2), October 2006, pp. 397–425.

17. A provocative study published in 2004 documents one way that politicians may get their favors returned before leaving office. Four researchers examined the stock portfolios of U.S.

Senators between 1993 and 2001, and found that Senators that actively traded stocks were remarkably good at it: the companies they invested in often sharply increased in value in the months that followed. Maybe politicians are good at timing financial markets. Or maybe they knew something about the future profitability of these companies before the rest of us. See A. J. Ziobrowski, P. Cheng, J. W. Boyd, and B. J. Ziobrowski, "Abnormal Returns from the Common Stock Investments of Members of the United States Senate," *Journal of Financial and Quantitative Analysis*, 39(4), December 2004, pp. 661–76.

18. David Fisman, Ray Fisman, Julia Galef, and Rakesh Khurana (2006). "Estimating the value of political connections to Vice-President Cheney," unpublished manuscript Columbia University.

19. Halliburton is a generous donor to Republican political causes (see www.opensecrets.org for information on corporate contributions), and these donations may have bought Halliburton a host of ties in Washington. But this is still very different from the deeply personalized high-level corruption of Suharto's Indonesia.

CHAPTER 3: THE SMUGGLING GAP

1. Interested readers should refer to Gary Becker's seminal discussion of the economics of crime, "Crime and Punishment: An Economic Approach," in the *Journal of Political Economy* (1968). For a review of various factors affecting criminal behaviors, refer to Steve Levitt's (2004). "Understanding Why Crime Fell in the 1990s: Four Factors that Explain the Decline and Six that Do Not," *Journal of Economic Perspectives*, 18(1), pp. 163–90.

2. Refer to Marc Levinson (2006). *The Box* (Princeton: Princeton University Press).

3. One obvious way of cracking down on handbag smugglers would be to have some communication between the Italian and American customs agents. However, for the most part there is very little of this sort of cooperation. And if there were such collabora-

tion, more people would presumably start lying to the Italian customs officials, too.

4. By 2004, the gap had narrowed to only 0.3 percent, as China brought down its overall tariff level to gain entry into the World Trade Organization.

5. Raymond Fisman and Shang-Jin Wei (2004). "Tax Rates and Tax Evasion: Evidence from 'Missing Imports' in China," *Journal of Political Economy* 112(2).

6. This is conceptually similar to what some economists call the Laffer Curve, where increasing tax rates above some point actually lead to less government revenue.

7. With the help of his government connections, Lai escaped to Canada where he has lived under house arrest since 2002. He continues to fight extradition to China where he would almost certainly receive a death sentence, the punishment meted out to the fourteen senior government officials implicated in his smuggling operation. See "Smuggler's Blues" by Hannah Beech (October 7, 2002, *Time*), and "Big Smuggling Ring with a Wide Reach Scandalizes China," *New York Times*, Jan. 22, 2000, by Erik Eckholm, for brief accounts of Mr. Lai's rise and fall.

8. See "Umbrian Umbrage: Send Back That Etruscan Chariot," *New York Times*, April 5, 2007.

9. In recent years, the U.S. government has signed bilateral treaties with some countries that make it illegal to import cultural objects that were exported illegally. However, this still only applies to a relatively small subset of countries and objects.

10. Raymond Fisman and Shang-jin Wei (2007). "The Smuggling of Art, and the Art of Smuggling: Uncovering the Illicit Trade in Cultural Property and Antiques," *National Bureau of Economic Research* working paper 13446.

11. For more information, see the *Doing Business Report 2008* (http://www.doingbusiness.org/).

12. See "Steel Smugglers Pull Wool Over the Eyes Of Customs Agents to Enter U.S. Market," *Wall Street Journal*, November 1, 2001.

13. See "In Apparel, All Tariffs Aren't Created Equal," *New York Times*, April 28, 2007.

CHAPTER 4: NATURE OR NURTURE?

1. For a media account of Mockus's rule, refer to John Rockwell (2004). "Reverberations: Where Mimes Patrolled the Streets and the Mayor was Superman," *New York Times*, July 9, 2004.

2. See "Academic turns city into a social experiment," by Maria Caballero in the *Harvard Gazette*, March 11, 2004. This article provides a summary of Mr. Mockus's lecture at Harvard's Institute of Politics in January, 2004.

3. The parking violations analysis is based on our joint paper, Raymond Fisman and Edward Miguel, "Corruption, Norms and Legal Enforcement: Evidence from Diplomatic Parking Tickets," (2008). *Journal of Political Economy*, 115(6).

4. To be absolutely clear, throughout this chapter we are talking about diplomats representing their home countries in U.N. missions. We do not have parking data on the permanent U.N. staff—though that would be fodder for another interesting study.

5. We gratefully acknowledge the New York City Department of Finance, in particular Sam Miller and Gerald Koszner, for compiling these data. We are also grateful to Gillian Sorensen, former New York City Commissioner for United Nations and Consular Affairs, for a helpful discussion.

6. See the paper by Dani Kaufmann, Aart Kraay, and Massimo Mastruzzi, "Governance Matters V: Governance Indicators for 1996–2005" for further details on this measure. Available on the World Bank website at http://info.worldbank.org/governance/wgi2007/pdf/govmatters5.pdf (last accessed March 23, 2008).

7. "U.N. Hears of 2 Diplomats' Treatment," *New York Times*, January 10, 1997.

8. This has started to change in recent years, thanks to the pioneering efforts of a renegade band of "behavioral economists" including Matthew Rabin and Nobel Prize winner George Akerlof, both at University of California, Berkeley. Their research shows how people's feelings—say, about fairness or about identity—can drive economic decision making just as powerfully as the financial incentives that dominate standard economic analysis.

9. There is more discussion of this result in the working paper

version, "Cultures of Corruption: Evidence from Diplomatic Parking Tickets," NBER Working Paper #12312 (2006).

10. Baltic News Service, "Estonia's UN diplomats less law-abiding than neighboring countries–study," July 10, 2006.

11. For media accounts of the diplomatic parking saga in New York City, refer to Jacob H. Fries. "U.S. Revokes License Plates Issued to 185 at 30 Consulates," *New York Times*, September 7, 2002; Jennifer Steinhauer. "Suspension of Hostilities Over Diplomats' Tickets," *New York Times*, August 23, 2002; and Don Singleton. "Bill Socks Scofflaw Diplos," *New York Daily News*, November 21, 2004, p. 28.

CHAPTER 5: No WATER, No PEACE

1. See Senan Murray, "Lake Chad Fishermen Pack up their Nets," *BBC News Website*, published Jan. 15, 2007.

2. For those interested in the actual data, check out the International Peace Research Institute of Oslo (PRIO) website at http://new.prio.no/CSCW-Datasets/Data-on-Armed-Conflict/Uppsala PRIO-Armed-Conflicts-Dataset/ (last visited March 29, 2008), and in particular their Armed Conflicts Dataset. Our claims about civil war patterns in this chapter are predominantly drawn from Version 4-2006b of this dataset.

3. L. Roberts, P. Ngoy, C. Mone, C. Lubula, L. Mwezse (2003). "Mortality in the Democratic Republic of Congo: Results from a nationwide survey." International Rescue Committee, New York.

4. James Fearon and David Laitin (2003), "Ethnicity, Insurgency, and Civil War," *American Political Science Review*, 97 (March), is a leading academic reference on the subject.

5. Data on coffee prices can be found at the International Coffee Organization website www.ico.org (refer to the data series "Historical Data: Prices paid to growers in exporting countries").

6. See L. Roberts, R Lafta, R Garfield, J Khudhairi (2004). "Mortality before and after the 2003 invasion of Iraq: cluster sample survey," *Lancet*, 364(9448), pp. 1857–64. Not surprisingly, this report too sparked controversy (see Michael Spagat, Neil Johnson, Sean Gourley, Jukka-Pekka Onnela, and Gesine Reinart [2007],

"Bias in Epidemiological Studies of Conflict Mortality," HiCN Research Design Note 2).

7. For information on the sometimes irregular census dates of African countries, refer to the U.S. Census Bureau website: http://www.census.gov/ipc/www/cendates/cenafric.html (last visited March 29, 2008).

8. We focus here on the time period from 1981 to 1999, the period examined in the Miguel, Satyanath, and Sergenti (2004) paper, "Economic Shocks and Civil Conflict: An Instrumental Variables Approach," *Journal of Political Economy*, 112(4).

9. BBC News, August 15, 2005. "Drought Diary V: Avoiding disaster in Mali," Mark Snelling.

10. Miguel, Satyanath, and Sergenti (2004). "Economic Shocks and Civil Conflict: An Instrumental Variables Approach."

11. Ibid. We use the Global Precipitation Climatology Project (GPCP) database. The GPCP data are publicly available at http://orbit-net.nesdis.noaa.gov/arad/gpcp/. We focus on the period 1981 to 1999, when the satellite data and all other variables in the analysis were available.

12. The relationship between cold cloud cover and rainfall is first estimated in areas where ground gauges are in place. Then once that relationship is known, rainfall can be estimated even in areas without reliable ground stations, like much of rural Africa. In this way, satellite technology allows us to fill in the gaps on the map.

13. Variability here is measured as the coefficient of variation in annual rainfall from the GPCP data, a standard statistical metric.

14. H. Kazianga and C. Udry (2006). "Consumption Smoothing? Livestock, Insurance, and Drought in Rural Burkina Faso," *Journal of Development Economics*, 79, pp. 413–46.

15. David Bloom and Jeffrey Sachs (1998), "Geography, Demography, and Economic Growth in Africa," *Brookings Papers on Economic Activity*, 2, p. 222.

16. Monique Mekenkamp, Paul van Tongeren, and Hans van de Veen (1999). *Searching for Peace in Africa: An Overview of Conflict Prevention and Management Activities* (Utrecht: European

Platform for Conflict Prevention and Transformation), p. 326. On the 2004 Niger drought, refer to http://www.reliefweb.int/rw/RWB.NSF/db900SID/DPAS-6N5HX3?OpenDocument (last visited March 29, 2008).

17. *New York Times*, "World Briefing: Africa: Niger: Rebel Attack at Army Base Kills 13," June 23, 2007.

18. The International Energy Agency Statistics, 2007 (www.iea.org) contains detailed global data on CO_2 emissions.

19. The full report can be found at: http://www.ipcc.ch/ (last visited March 29, 2008). Much of the research in this section is based on ongoing joint work with John Dykema and Shanker Satyanath. We are especially grateful to John Dykema for many insightful conversations on climate models.

20. This is for the range of low emission to high emission scenarios: see http://ipcc-wg1.ucar.edu/wg1/wg1-report.html, p. 13 (last visited March 29, 2008).

21. There is no single accepted definition of the Sahel. The following organizations have different definitions: USAID (http://www.usaid.gov/press/factsheets/2005/fs050803.html), the Community of Sahel-Saharan States (http://www.africa-union.org/root/au/RECs/cen_sad.htm), and the International Development Research Centre (http://www.idrc.ca/en/ev-43109-201-1-DO_TOPIC.html). A reasonable definition of the Sahel includes parts of the following fifteen countries: Burkina Faso, Cape Verde, Chad, Djibouti, Eritrea, Ethiopia, Gambia, Guinea-Bissau, Mali, Mauritania, Niger, Nigeria, Senegal, Somalia, and Sudan. The per capita GDP figure in the text is population weighted for these countries (minus Somalia, which has no reliable national income figures for recent years) and comes from the World Development Indicators Online (http://devdata.worldbank.org/wdi2006/contents/cover.htm). The climate estimates for the Sahel come from a convenient geographic rectangle bounded between 4 to 2° north latitude and 13° west and 17° east longitude (websites last visited March 29, 2008).

22. The view that a lack of rainfall is driving the Darfur conflict has recently been challenged by Michael Kevane and Leslie Gray (2007), "Rainfall in Darfur Prior to the Conflict in

2003," in a paper presented at the Working Group in African Political Economy meeting at Stanford University in December 2007.

23. For two contrasting media accounts, see two BBC (news. bbc.co.uk) articles from July 2007: "Water find 'may end Darfur war,'" July 18, 2007, and "Ancient Darfur lake 'is dried up,'" July 20, 2007.

CHAPTER 6: DEATH BY A THOUSAND CUTS

1. For the first formal theoretical discussion of this idea within economics, refer to J. A.Mirrlees (1975). "A Pure Theory of Underdeveloped Economies," in L. Reynolds (ed.). *Agriculture in Development Theory* (New Haven: Yale University Press).

2. Michael Brogden (2000). *Geronticide: Killing the Elderly* (London: Jessica Kingsley Publishers), p. 65.

3. Peter Geschiere (1997). Translated by P. Geschiere and J. Roitman. *The Modernity of Witchcraft: Politics and the Occult in Postcolonial Africa* (Charlottesville: University of Virginia Press), p. 11.

4. S. Mesaki (1994). "Witch-Killing in Sukumaland," in R. Abrahams (ed.). *Witchcraft in Contemporary Tanzania* (African Studies Center, University of Cambridge), p. 58.

5. Most of the research findings in this chapter are from Edward Miguel (2005). "Poverty and Witch Killing," *Review of Economic Studies*, 72(4), pp. 1153–72.

6. International crime statistics can be found at http://www .uncjin.org/Statistics/WCTS/wcts.html (last visited March 29, 2008).

7. Refer to British Broadcasting Corporation (BBC). (2001). "Ghana 'Witch' Sues Village Elders," April 6, 2001, BBC News Online; Elisha Otieno (2003), "Couple Lynched over Witchcraft," *The Daily Nation (Nairobi)*, August 19, 2003, p. 7; Isak Niehaus (2001). "Witchcraft in the new South Africa: From Colonial Superstition to Post-Colonial Reality?," in Henrietta Moore and Todd Sanders (eds.). *Magical Interpretations and Material Realities: Modernity, Witchcraft and the Occult in Postcolonial Africa* (London: Routledge).

8. "African Crucible: Cast as Witches, Then Cast Out," *New York Times*, November 15, 2007.

9. For the seminal reference on the economic causes of European witch hunts, see Wolfgang Behringer. (1999). "Climatic Change and Witch-Hunting: The Impact of the Little Ice Age on Mentalities," *Climatic Change*, 43, pp. 335–51. Also refer to Emily Oster (2004). "Witchcraft, Weather and Economic Growth in Medieval Europe," *Journal of Economic Perspectives*, 18(1), pp. 215–28.

10. Rena Singer (2000). "Anti-Witch Hunting Laws Create Tension in South Africa," *Christian Science Monitor*, Dec. 6, 2000. Of course, many other things were also changing in South Africa at the time, especially the end of Apartheid, making it hard to pin down exactly what brought the witch killing to an end.

11. Maia Green (2003). *Priests, Witches, and Power: Popular Christiantiy After Mission in Southern Tanzania* (New York: Cambridge Studies in Social and Cultural Anthropology, Cambridge University Press).

12. Ibid., p. 126.

13. For more on Mungiki, refer to BBC, "Profile: Kenya's Secret Mungiki Sect," May 24, 2007; and Jeffrey Gettleman, "Might Drink Your Blood, but Otherwise Not Bad Guys," *New York Times*, June 22, 2007.

14. Ted first coined this term in his 2007 piece, "Poverty and Violence: An Overview of Recent Research and Implications for Foreign Aid," in *Too Poor for Peace? Global Poverty, Conflict and Security in the 21st Century*, Lael Brainard and Derek Chollet (eds.) (Washington, D.C.: Brookings Institution Press), 2007. See also his piece in *Businessweek*, "Stop Conflict Before it Starts," September 18, 2006. Ted thanks Dr. Rachel Glennerster for useful early conversations about RCPS.

15. Recent research finds this relationship between commodity price changes and civil war in sub-Saharan Africa. See "Growth, Democracy, and Civil War," by Markus Bruckner and Antonio Ciccone, unpublished working paper Universitat Pompeu Fabra.

16. This is the Famine Early Warning System (http://www. fews.net/).

17. Refer to Theodore Valentine (1993). "Drought, Transfers, Entitlements and Income Distribution: The Botswana Experience." *World Development*, 21(1), pp. 109–26.

18. This conversation took place on August 2, 2007 in Aspen, Colorado, at the Brookings-Blum Roundtable examining "The Tangled Web: Breaking the Poverty-Insecurity Nexus" conference.

19. For a comparison of Kenya and Tanzania, refer to Edward Miguel (2004). "Tribe or Nation? Nation-Building and Public Goods in Kenya versus Tanzania," *World Politics*, 56(3), pp. 327–62.

20. The most closely related academic discussion of foreign aid and conflict prevention, to our knowledge, is Paul Collier and Anke Hoeffler (2002). "Aid, Policy and Peace: Reducing the Risks of Civil Conflict," *Defense and Peace Economics*, 13, pp. 435–50. These researchers also argue that an increase in foreign aid is likely to reduce civil conflict risk, and they empirically demonstrate some modest reductions in conflict for aid recipients, working through the channel of faster economic growth. Yet they study the effect of existing foreign aid instruments on conflict, rather than aid with the monitoring mechanisms, forward-looking timing, and targeting in the RCPS proposal.

21. For a range of popular media articles on the Chad-Cameroon pipeline, refer to the following websites: http://www.ciel.org/Ifi/chadcameroonproject.html: http://www.csmonitor.com/2006/0421/p06s01-woaf.html; http://www.pbs.org/wnet/religionandethics/week543/cover.html; www.worldbank.org/afr/ccproj (last visited March 29, 2008).

CHAPTER 7: THE ROAD BACK FROM WAR

1. *Agence France Press*, April 3, 1995.

2. Michael Clodfelter (1995). *Vietnam in Military Statistics: A History of the Indochina Wars 1772–1991* (Jefferson, NC: McFarland).

3. Unfortunately, we have only rudimentary information on the location of unexploded bombs, untriggered land mines, and

the use of the herbicide/defoliant Agent Orange. But we can reasonably assume that the number of still-active explosives in any given location is very closely related to the quantity of bombs that were dropped there during the war.

4. The U.S. Department of Energy page contains a discussion; see: http://www.cfo.doe.gov/me70/manhattan/hiroshima.htm and http://www.cfo.doe.gov/me70/manhattan/nagasaki.htm (last visited March 29, 2008).

5. Donald Davis and David Weinstein (2002). "Bones, Bombs, and Breakpoints: The Geography of Economic Activity," *American Economic Review*, 92(5).

6. Districts are administrative units similar to U.S. counties; a district typically contains several hundred villages.

7. For the curious reader, this result didn't change in the analysis when we measured bombing intensity in different ways, looked at larger administrative units (provinces instead of districts), and used statistical "control" variables, like prewar population density and geographic factors; see Miguel and Roland (2006), "The Long Run Impact of Bombing Vietnam", NBER Working Paper #11954, for the details.

8. Earl H. Tilford, Jr. (1991). *Setup: What the Air Force Did in Vietnam and Why* (Maxwell Air Force Base, AL: Air University Press).

9. Source: World Development Indicators (http://devdata. worldbank.org/wdi2006/contents/cover.htm, last visited March 29, 2008.

10. Source: Human Development Report 2006 online (http:// hdr.undp.org/en/reports/global/hdr2006/, last visited March 29, 2008).

11. See Charles Tilly (1975). *The Formation of National States in Western Europe* (Princeton, NJ: Princeton University Press). For a related recent African example, refer to Jeffrey Gettleman, "Resentment and Rations as Eritrea Nears a Crisis," *New York Times*, October 16, 2007. Vietnam's war is actually a more complicated story, as it combined an external army (the U.S.-led coalition) and elements of a civil war, but the postwar political rhetoric of the victorious Communist North emphasized the former.

12. This is a historical irony since Republicans led the Union during the Civil War and were reviled in the South for decades afterwards.

13. A notable exception is Anke Hoeffler and Paul Collier (2007). "Chapter 3: Civil War," *Handbook of Defense Economics 2*, eds. Todd Sandler and Keith Hartley (North Holland), which lays out the research that has been done on these topics.

14. When asked in 1984 if he was disturbed by any of this, Stevens replied, "I am disturbed, but that is the way the world is built." See "In Sierra Leone, Land of Diamonds, Decay Sets in," *New York Times*, June 21, 1984.

15. Source: Sierra Leone News Archives, June 3, 2003: www .sierra-leone.org/slnews0603.html (last visited March 29, 2008).

16. Interested readers should refer to David Keen (2005). *Conflict and Collusion in Sierra Leone* (London: James Currey; New York: Palgrave); and John Bellows and Edward Miguel (2008). "War and Institutions: New Evidence from Sierre Leone," *American Economic Review*, 96(2), pp. 394–99.

17. Fox News commentator William Kristol provides a concise statement of this view in an April 1, 2003 interview with Terri Gross on National Public Radio.

18. M. Guidolin and E. La Ferrara (2007). "Diamonds are forever, wars are not: Is conflict bad for private firms?," *American Economic Review*, 97(5).

19. The Angola Peace Monitor: http://www.actsa.org/Pages/ Page.php?pID=1084&title=Angola%20Peace%20Monitor (last visited March 29, 2008).

20. The discussion in this textbox has been published as a column in Slate, at http://www.slate.com/id/2172333/ (last visited May 29, 2008).

CHAPTER 8: LEARNING TO FIGHT ECONOMIC GANGSTERS

1. These data come from the *World Development Indicators*, an annual database compiled by the World Bank.

2. BBC News Africa, "Huge pay rise for Kenya's police," January 22, 2004.

3. See, for example, the World Bank's *Doing Business 2007* report which includes, in addition to a general discussion on wages and corruption, a detailed description of reforms in the country Georgia and the role played by higher salaries in these reforms.

4. For perhaps the most detailed recent study of these programs, interested readers should refer to Macartan Humphreys and Jeremy Weinstein (2007). "Demobilization and reintegration," *Journal of Conflict Resolution*, 51(4), pp. 531–67.

5. While the medical community today accepts the use of randomized trials for evaluating new treatments, quite surprisingly, this is a relatively recent development. The idea has been around since at least since 1652, when it was proposed by a Dutch medicinal chemist as a means of determining whether he was better at healing patients than his doctor colleagues (his challenge was not accepted). But in the hierarchical medical establishment, senior physicians dictated dogma from on high, and were understandably resistant to having their position of power challenged by upstarts armed with objective scientific evidence. David Wootton's 2006 book, *Bad Medicine: Doctors Doing Harm Since Hippocrates* (New York: Oxford University Press) describes the long struggle to establish more scientific medical practices through the ages. See also Jerome Groopman (2007). *How Doctors Think* (Boston: Houghton Mifflin).

6. Interested readers should refer to Esther Duflo, Michael Kremer, and Rachel Glennerster's (2008) *Handbook of Development Economics Volume 4*, eds. T. Paul Schultz and John Strauss (North Holland) chapter "Using Randomization in Development Economics Research: A Toolkit" for a detailed discussion of the method, as well as a discussion of seminal randomized experimental studies within economics, including Robert J. Lalonde's (1986) piece, "Evaluating the Econometric Evaluations of Training Programs Using Experimental Data," *American Economic Review*, 76(4), pp. 602–20. The Mexican Progresa program was a pioneering use of randomized evaluation within development economics, see T. Paul Schultz (2004). "School subsidies for the poor: evaluating Mexico's Progresa poverty program," *Journal of Development Economics*, 74(1), pp. 199–250.

7. Ted and Michael's main nonprofit collaborator is currently Innovations for Poverty Action (website: http://www.poverty-action.org/). The MIT J-PAL's website is: http://www.povertylab.com/. We are grateful to Dr. Rachel Glennerster, Director of J-PAL, for many useful discussions.

8. The academic paper is Edward Miguel and Michael Kremer (2004). "Worms: Identifying Impacts on Education and Health in the Presence of Treatment Externalities," Econometrica, 72(1), pp. 159–217. This and all the other Busia studies can also be found on the J-PAL website. Nicholas Kristof featured our deworming results in his New York Times column on July 2, 2007 ("Attack of the Worms").

9. Researchers in Busia have also recently used randomized evaluation to assess which types of sex education lessons are most effective in preventing pregnancy and sexually transmitted diseases among young African schoolgirls. In case you're wondering, traditional sex education doesn't reduce unsafe sex, but targeted lessons warning girls about older "sugar daddies" do. See Pascaline Dupas (2006), "Relative Risks and the Market for Sex: Teenagers, Sugar Daddies, and HIV in Kenya," unpublished working paper, Dartmouth University; and Esther Duflo, Pascaline Dupas, Michael Kremer, and Samuel Sinei (2006). "Education and HIV/AIDS Prevention: Evidence from a randomized evaluation in Western Kenya," World Bank Policy Research Working Paper #4024, June 2006.

10. Paul Glewwe, Michael Kremer, and Sylvie Moulin (2007). "Many Children Left Behind? Textbooks and Test Scores in Kenya," forthcoming American Economic Journal: Applied Economics.

11. UNICEF press release, "4.5 million children across Ghana to be deworming," February 5, 2007.

12. Ben Olken (2007). "Monitoring Corruption: Evidence from a Field Experiment in Indonesia," Journal of Political Economy, 115(2), pp. 200–49.

13. All academic research projects involving human subjects must be approved by a university's Institutional Review Board, to ensure that the ethical lapses of the past are not repeated today. This includes all of the Busia projects described above, as well as

the Olken and Gine-Yang studies. The early days of randomized clinical trials in medicine are littered with practices appalling to modern sensibilities. Among the most infamous is the Willowbrook experiment, where residents of an institution for the mentally retarded were deliberately infected with hepatitis B as part of a vaccine trial. An active and healthy debate continues on how to best ensure that experiments are performed in an ethical manner. See, for example, "Guinea-pigging," by Carl Elliott in *The New Yorker*, January 7, 2008.

14. For a concise statement of the MVP's activities in Sauri, refer to the Executive Summary document, "The Millenium Villages: A New Approach to Fighting Poverty—Sauri, Kenya: Highlights of Success 2004–2006," found online on June 21, 2007 at: http://www.earth.columbia.edu/millenniumvillages/Sauri_ Executive_Summary.php. For a more critical external look at the MVP in Sauri, refer to Victoria Schlesinger's "The continuation of poverty: Rebranding foreign aid in Kenya," *Harper's Magazine*, May 2007.

15. The Sauri research team has collected surveys from local residents on an impressive array of topics. Thanks to these data collection efforts, we now know, for example, about the tripling of corn production after only one year.

16. This figure comes from The Millennium Villages Project *Baseline Report Millennium Research Village Sauri, Kenya*, February 7, 2007, Table 1 (p. 10).

17. The Millennium Villages Project *Annual Report for Sauri, Kenya Millennium Research Village*, November 29, 2006, claims there were "heavy rains" in 2005 (p. 3). NOAA also reports on the heavy rainfall in western Kenya in 2005: http://www.ncdc.noaa .gov/oa/climate/research/2005/may/hazards.html (last visited March 29, 2008).

Index

The letters *b*, *n*, and *t* refer to boxes, notes, and tables on the pages indicated. The number following an *n* refers to the note number on that page.

Chad (*continued*)
  global warming and, 131; Lake
    Chad, 111–12; paperwork delays
    in, 66–67; petroleum deposits
    in, 155–58; political turmoil
    in, 112–13; rainfall and, 114;
    violence in, 175; World Bank
    and, 156–58
cheap talk, 18–20; violence and,
  118b–19b
Cheney, Dick, 29, 51–52
China: 1998 anticorruption
  campaign and, 70–73; global
  warming and, 127–29; smuggling and, 55–57; tariffs and,
  60–64, 221n4, 221n6
China National Petroleum Company (CNPC), 185b
Clodfelter, Michael, 160–61
coffee, 117–18, 149–50
Collier, Paul, 215n9, 228n20,
  230n13
Colombia, 76–78, 102–3, 142
commodity prices, 117–18, 149–50,
  227n15
conflict traps, Chad and, 113–14
containerization, 56–57
corruption: bottom line on,
  102–3; cheap talk and, 18–20;
  culture and, 80–81, 87, 102–3;
  definition of, 18, 83, 216n12;
  economic growth and, 41–46;
  income level and, 91–92;
  measuring, stock markets
  and, 24–29; national pride
  and, 100–102; outsiders and,
  41–43; poverty and, 15–17;
  "Scramble for Africa" and,
  101–2; stock markets and,
  24–27; wages and, 189, 230n3.

  See also specific countries;
    under culture
  costs versus benefits, 54–55,
    56–57, 78
crime, organization and, 43b–46b
culture: corruption and, 78–80,
  87, 102; violence and, 137. *See
  also specific countries*

Darfur, 115; rainfall and, 135b,
  225n22; underground lake in,
  134b–35b
data, war and, 118b–20b
Davis, Don, 162
Deby, Idriss, 157–58
Democratic Republic of Congo,
  115–16
deworming, 193–95
diamond mining, Angola,
  181b–85b
diplomatic immunity, 82–84, 222n4
Duflo, Esther, 231n6

Easterly, Bill, 12–15; *White Man's
  Burden*, 13–14
economic development: corruption
  and, 41–43; fighting for, 1–3
economic gangsters, 5–8, 215n6.
  *See also specific individuals and
  situations*
economic growth, corruption and,
  41–46
el-Baz, Farouk, 135
End of Poverty (Sachs), 11
Enron, 37
Estonia, 101
Ethiopia, 9

Faccio, Mara, 47–48
famine: migration and, 137; selec-